W9-AMQ-528

## FURTHER INVESTIGATION
## OF LIFE AFTER LIFE

Dr. Moody has continued his research into near-death experiences since the publication of *Life After Life*. He has now interviewed hundreds more men and women who were close to death or actually pronounced dead. New elements not encountered in *Life After Life* case histories are recorded here for the first time. As evidence of the afterlife mounts, Dr. Moody brings us one step closer to unraveling mankind's greatest mystery.

Bantam Books by Dr. Raymond A. Moody

LIFE AFTER LIFE
REFLECTIONS ON LIFE AFTER LIFE

Reflections On
# LIFE
# AFTER
# LIFE

by Raymond A. Moody, Jr., M.D.

BANTAM BOOKS
TORONTO • NEW YORK • LONDON • SYDNEY • AUCKLAND

REFLECTIONS ON LIFE AFTER LIFE
*A Bantam Book published by
arrangement with Mockingbird Books*

*PRINTING HISTORY*
*Bantam / Mockingbird edition / June 1977*
*Bantam edition / March 1978*

| | | |
|---|---|---|
| *2nd printing . . . . March 1978* | *4th printing . . . . . . May 1978* |
| *3rd printing . . . . . April 1978* | *5th printing . . . . . . June 1982* |
| | *6th printing . . . November 1983* | |

*All rights reserved.*
*Copyright © 1977 by Raymond A. Moody, Jr.*
*This book may not be reproduced in whole or in part, by
mimeograph or any other means, without permission.
For information address: Mockingbird Books, Box 624,
St. Simons Island, Georgia 31522.*

ISBN 0-553-24148-6

*Published simultaneously in the United States and Canada*

Bantam Books are published by Bantam Books, Inc. Its trademark, consisting of the words "Bantam Books" and the portrayal of a rooster, is registered in U.S. Patent and Trademark
Office and in other countries. Marca Registrada. Bantam
Books, Inc., 666 Fifth Avenue, New York, New York 10103.

PRINTED IN THE UNITED STATES OF AMERICA

H    15 14 13 12 11 10 9 8 7

*With Love*
*for Elisabeth,*
*who has helped us see the way*
*and for Vi, Andy, and Dannion,*
*three who came back*

Abraham saith unto him, They have Moses and the prophets; let them hear them. And he said, Nay, father Abraham; but if one went unto them from the dead, they will repent. And he said unto him, If they hear not Moses and the prophets, neither will they be persuaded, though one rose from the dead.

*Luke 16:29-31*

Strange, is it not? that of the
   myriads who
Before us passed the door of
   Darkness through,
Not one returns to tell us of the
   Road,
Which to discover we must
   travel too.

*The Rubáiyát of Omar Khayyám*

# Acknowledgments

This book was in preparation for a period of well over a year, and in that time many people and institutions have aided me in conceiving and planning it. First of all, I would like to thank the many hundreds of people who have told or written me of their spiritual experiences as they faced imminent death. The comments, questions, suggestions, and references to related literature which so many people have so kindly taken the time to write to me have been greatly appreciated.

Elisabeth Kubler-Ross, M.D., has given encouragement to go on with the work of discussing with persons their close calls with death. Ian Stevenson, M.D., has helped by reviewing and commenting on the section on methodology. George Ritchie, M.D., read the manuscript and made valuable remarks, even at a time when he was busy, not only with his own practice, but also with the task of writing a book about his own experience. Beverley Belk, M.D., has drawn upon her own practical wisdom and clinical acumen to make many interesting suggestions about how studies of this phenomenon might be carried out. John Audette spent considerable time in the library finding literature on the subject of this book, and in preparing a bibliography.

Very special thanks go to John Egle of Mockingbird Books, for helping in ways too numerous to list. Last but not least, I want to express my appreciation to my wife, Louise, and my two sons, for everything they have done in the way of making this volume possible.

# Contents

# INTRODUCTION

The present volume, which is intended to be read in conjunction with my previous book, *Life After Life*, represents an extension of and an addition to some of the concepts and findings discussed there.

Since the publication of *Life After Life*, I have had the opportunity to interview many more people who have had near-death experiences. As a matter of fact, I am now uncovering new cases of this phenomenon so rapidly that I am no longer keeping track of the exact number. As in my previous study, some of these people were actually pronounced clinically dead, while others only came very close to death in the course of a serious injury or accident. In the mass of material which has resulted, the fifteen common elements discussed in *Life After Life* have continued to recur. In addition, I have encountered some new and unusual experiences which seem to expand the list of elements.

For years I had wondered why, if these experiences *were* as common as I had found them to be, other people weren't also collecting reports of them. I felt that when I reported on my research, it might be thought that I was fabricating all this. Indeed, it even occurred to me that maybe this was not a widespread phenomenon, that perhaps, by some wild chain of coincidences, I had stumbled upon the *only* cases of this experience which there were or ever would be. This was a frightening thought to me in that in writing *Life After Life* I was banking heavily on a kind of repeatability—that is, that any sympathetic and diligent investigator could find an ample number of cases for himself.

Interestingly, many recent developments have settled a lot of my anxiety about this. I have found that several other physicians—most notably Dr. Elisabeth Kubler-Ross—have been pursuing this same research and have been getting identical accounts. In fact, when Dr. Kubler-Ross received pre-publication proofs of my first book, she wrote my publisher that she could have written the same manuscript herself on the basis of what she had been doing. She states that she now has hundreds of reports of this kind, and she is in the process of preparing a major book on the subject. Numerous doctors and ministers have also told me that they had long been noticing isolated cases of this phenomenon and felt that it might be quite prevalent.

When I gave talks on this subject in the past, individuals who had experienced near-death phenomena came forward only privately afterward. However, I have noticed in recent months a new openness and willingness to talk. Some people have now been relating their experiences publicly and unsolicitedly during the discussion periods which follow my lectures. Thus, many others have now had the experience of actually hearing firsthand from people who have been close to death and of sensing something of the warmth and sincerity that I have found in these accounts.

On the basis of these and many other similar developments, I can now say with confidence that this phenomenon—whatever it ultimately means —is a widespread one. Indeed, it is so widespread that I believe that very soon the question will not be whether there really is such a phenomenon but rather, "What are we to make of it?" One of the points of *Life After Life* was simply to introduce the phenomenon and to predict that if others were interested, they, too, could find instances of it. It now appears that many others are interested in studying near-death experiences.

As a beginning, then, to this new volume, let me restate the theoretically complete model experience which I first constructed in *Life After Life*. It embodies all of the common elements of typical near-death experiences.

*A man is dying and, as he reaches the point of greatest physical distress, he hears himself pronounced dead by his doctor. He begins to hear an uncomfortable noise, a loud ringing or buzzing, and at the same time feels himself moving very rapidly through a long tunnel. After this, he suddenly finds himself outside of his own physical body, but still in the immediate physical environment, and he sees his own body from a distance, as though he is a spectator. He watches the resus-*

*citation attempt from this unusual vantage point and is in a state of emotional upheaval.*

*After a while, he collects himself and becomes more accustomed to his odd condition. He notices that he still has a "body," but one of a very different nature and with very different powers from the physical body he has left behind. Soon other things begin to happen. Others come to meet and to help him. He glimpses the spirits of relatives and friends who have already died, and a loving, warm spirit of a kind he has never encountered before—a being of light—appears before him. This being asks him a question, non-verbally, to make him evaluate his life and helps him along by showing him a panoramic, instantaneous playback of the major events of his life. At some point he finds himself approaching some sort of barrier or border, apparently representing the limit between earthly life and the next life. Yet, he finds that he must go back to the earth, that the time for his death has not yet come. At this point he resists, for by now he is taken up with his experiences in the afterlife and does not want to return. He is overwhelmed by intense feelings of joy, love, and peace. Despite his attitude, though, he somehow reunites with his physical body and lives.*

*Later he tries to tell others, but he has trouble doing so. In the first place, he can find no human words adequate to describe these unearthly episodes. He also finds that others scoff, so he stops telling other people. Still, the experience affects his life profoundly, especially his views about death and its relationship to life.*

# 1
# NEW ELEMENTS

In the process of studying the large number of accounts of near-death experiences which I have collected since the completion of *Life After Life*, I have encountered several new elements which were not included there. Each of the elements I will discuss in this chapter has been reported to me by more than one person, but they are far from being as common as the original fifteen. With the exception of the "supernatural rescues," all of these unusual elements occurred exclusively in the reports of subjects who had near-death encounters of extreme duration.

## The Vision of Knowledge

Several people have told me that during their encounters with "death," they got brief glimpses of an entire separate realm of existence in which all knowledge—whether of past, present, or future —seemed to co-exist in a sort of timeless state. Alternately, this has been described as a moment of enlightenment in which the subject seemed to have complete knowledge. In trying to talk about this aspect of their experience, all have commented that this experience was ultimately inexpressible. Also, all agree that this feeling of complete knowledge did not persist after their return; that they did not bring back any sort of omniscience. They agree that this vision did not discourage them from trying to learn in this life, but, rather, encouraged them to do so.

The experience has been compared, in various accounts, to a flash of universal insight, institutions of higher learning, a "school," and a "library." Everyone emphasizes, however, that the words they are using to describe this experience are at best only dim reflections of the reality they are trying to express. It is my own feeling that there may be one underlying state of consciousness which is at the root of all these different accounts.

One woman who had "died" gave the following report during an extended interview.

*You mentioned earlier that you seemed to have "a vision of knowledge," if I could call it that. Could you tell me about it?*

This seems to have taken place after I had seen my life pass before me. It seemed that all of a sudden, all knowledge—of all that had started from the very beginning, that would go on without end—that for a second I knew all the secrets of all ages, all the meaning of the universe, the stars, the moon—of everything. But after I chose to return, this knowledge escaped, and I can't remember any of it. It seems that when I made the decision [to return] I was told that I would not retain the knowledge. But I kept being called back by my children. . . .

This all-powerful knowledge opened before me. It seemed that I was being told that I was going to remain sick for quite a while and that I would have other close calls. And I did have several close calls after that. They said some of it would be to erase this all-knowing knowledge that I had picked up . . . that I had been granted the universal secrets and that I would have to undergo time to forget that knowledge. But I do have the memory of once knowing everything, that it did happen, but that it was not a gift that I would keep if I returned. But I chose to return to my children. . . . The memory of all these things that happened has remained clear, all except for that fleeting moment of knowledge. And that feeling of all knowledge disappeared when I returned to my body.

It sounds silly! Well, it does when you say it out loud . . . or it does to me, because I've never been able to sit and talk to someone else about it.

I don't know how to explain it, but I knew. . . . As *The Bible* says, "To you all things will be revealed." For a minute, there was no question that didn't have an answer. How long I knew it, I couldn't say. It wasn't in earthly time, anyway.

*In what form did this knowledge seem to be presented to you? Was it in words or pictures?*

It was in all forms of communication, sights, sounds, thoughts. It was any- and everything. It was as if there was nothing that wasn't known. All knowledge was there, not just of one field, but everything.

*One thing I wonder. I've spent a lot of my life seeking knowledge, learning. If this happens, isn't that sort of thing rather pointless?*

No! You still want to seek knowledge even after you come back here. I'm still seeking knowledge. . . . It's not silly to try to get the answers here. I sort of felt that it was part of our purpose . . . but that it wasn't just for one person, but that it was to be used for all mankind. We're always reaching out to help others with what we know.

There is one point which I would like to make here about this narrative. This woman plainly had the impression that part of the purpose of her lengthy recuperation was to make her forget almost all of the knowledge which had been revealed to her. This suggests that some mechanism was operative that had the function of blocking the knowledge acquired in this state of existence so that it could not be carried over into the physical state of being.

I am impressed by the similarity between this concept and one which was expressed—in an admittedly metaphorical and poetic way—by Plato in his telling of the story of Er, a warrior who came back to life on the funeral pyre, after having been believed dead. Er is said to have seen many things in the afterlife, but he was told that he must return to physical life to tell others what death is like. Just before he returned, he saw souls which were being prepared to be born into life:

They all journeyed to the Plain of Oblivion, through a terrible and stifling heat, for it was bare of trees and all plants, and there they camped at eventide by the River of Forgetfulness, whose waters no vessel can contain. They were all required to drink a measure of the water, and those who were not saved by their good sense drank more than the measure, and each one as he drank forgot all things. And after they had fallen asleep and it was the middle of the night, there was a sound of thunder and a quaking of the earth, and they were suddenly wafted thence, one this way, one that, upward to their birth like shooting stars. Er himself, he said, was not allowed to drink of the water, yet how and in what way he returned to the body he said he did not know, but suddenly recovering his sight he saw himself at dawn lying on the funeral pyre.[1]

The basic theme being presented here, that before returning to life a certain kind of "forgetting" of knowledge one has in the eternal state must take place, is similar in the two cases.

During another interview, a young man told me this:

Now, I was in a school . . . and it was real. It was not imaginary. If I were not absolutely sure, I would say, "Well, there is a possibility that I was in this place." But it *was* real. It was like a school, and there was no one there, and yet there were a lot of people there. Because if you looked around, you would *see* nothing . . . but if you paid attention, you would feel, sense, the presence of other beings around. . . . It's as if there were lessons coming at me and they would keep coming at me. . . .

*That's interesting. Another man told me that he went into what he called "libraries" and "institu-*

*tions of higher learning." Is that anything like what you're trying to tell me?*

Exactly! You see, hearing what you say he said about it, it's like I know exactly what he means, that I know he's been through this same thing I have. And, yet . . . the words I would use are different, because there really are no words . . . I cannot describe it. You could not compare it to anything here. The terms I'm using to describe it are so far from the thing, but it's the best I can do. . . . Because this is a place where the *place* is knowledge. . . . Knowledge and information are readily available—all knowledge. . . . You absorb knowledge. . . . You all of a sudden know the answers. . . . It's like you focus mentally on one place in that school and—zoom—knowledge flows by you from that place, automatically. It's just like you'd had about a dozen speed reading courses.

And I know verbatim what this man is talking about, but, you see, I'm just putting the same consciousness into my own words, which are different. . . .

I go on seeking knowledge; "Seek and ye shall find." You can get the knowledge for yourself. But I *pray* for wisdom, wisdom more than all. . . .

A middle-aged lady described it this way:

There was a moment in this thing—well, there isn't any way to describe it—but it was like I knew all things. . . . For a moment, there, it was like communication wasn't necessary. I thought whatever I wanted to know could be known.

## Cities of Light

I stated in *Life After Life* that I had not found any cases in which a "heaven"—at least in a certain traditional portrayal of that place—was described. However, I have now talked with numerous individuals who tell with remarkable consistency of catching glimpses of other realms of being which might well be termed "heavenly." It is interesting to me that in several of these accounts a single phrase—"a city of light"—occurs. In this and several other respects the imagery in which these scenes are described seems to be reminiscent of what is found in *The Bible*.

One middle-aged man who had a cardiac arrest related:

> I had heart failure and clinically died. . . . I remember everything perfectly vividly. . . . Suddenly I felt numb. Sounds began sounding a little distant. . . . All this time I was perfectly conscious of everything that was going on. I heard the heart monitor go off. I saw the nurse come into the room and dial the telephone, and the doctors, nurses, and attendants came in.
>
> As things began to fade there was a sound I can't describe; it was like the beat of a snare drum, very rapid, a rushing sound, like a stream rushing through a gorge. And I rose up and I was a few feet up looking down on my body. There I was, with people working on me. I had no fear. No pain. Just peace. After just probably a second or two, I seemed to turn over and go up. It was dark—you could call it a hole or a tunnel—and

there was this bright light. It got brighter and brighter. And I seemed to go *through* it.

All of a sudden I was just somewhere else. There was a gold-looking light, everywhere. Beautiful. I couldn't find a source anywhere. It was just all around, coming from everywhere. There was music. And I seemed to be in a countryside with streams, grass, and trees, mountains. But when I looked around—if you want to put it that way—they were not trees and things like we know them to be. The strangest thing to me about it was that there were people there. Not in any kind of form or body as we know it; they were just there.

There was a sense of perfect peace and contentment; love. It was like I was part of it. That experience could have lasted the whole night or just a second . . . I don't know.

Here's the way one woman described it:

There was a vibration of some sort. The vibration was surrounding me, all around my body. It was like the body vibrating, and where the vibration came from, I don't know. But when it vibrated, I became separated. I could then see my body. . . . I stayed around for a while and watched the doctor and nurses working on my body, wondering what would happen. . . . I was at the head of the bed, looking at them and my body, and at one time one nurse reached up to the wall over the bed to get the oxygen mask that was there and as she did she reached *through* my neck. . . .

And after I floated up, I went through this dark tunnel . . . I went into the black tunnel and came out into brilliant light. . . . A little bit later on I was there with my grandparents and my father and my brother, who had died. . . . There was the most beautiful, brilliant light all around. And this was a beautiful place. There were colors—bright colors—not like here on earth, but just indescribable. There were people there, happy people. . . . People were around, some of them gathered in groups. Some of them were learning. . . .

Off in the distance . . . I could see a city. There were buildings—separate buildings. They were gleaming, bright. People were happy in there. There was sparkling water, fountains . . . a city of light I guess would be the way to say it. . . . It was wonderful. There was beautiful music. Everything was just glowing, wonderful. . . . But if I had entered into this, I think I would never have returned. . . . I was told that if I went there I couldn't go back . . . that the decision was mine.

An elderly man said:

I was sitting in a chair. I started to get up and something hit me right in the chest. . . . I leaned against the wall. I sat down again, and then it hit me again, just like a sledge hammer hit me in the chest. . . . I was in the hospital . . . and they said I had a cardiac arrest. The doctor was right there.

*And what do you remember of your cardiac arrest?*

Well, it's a place . . . It's really beautiful, but you just can't describe it. But it's really there. You just can't imagine it. When you get on the other side, there's a river. Just like in *The Bible*, "There is a river. . . ." It had a smooth surface, just like glass. . . . Yeah, you cross a river. I did. . . .

*How did you feel you crossed this river?*

Walked. Just walked. But it was so pretty. It's beautiful. There's no way to describe it. We have beauty here, there's no question, with all these flowers and everything. But there is no comparison. It's so quiet over there and so peaceful. You feel like just resting. There was no darkness.

# A Realm of Bewildered Spirits

Several people have reported to me that at some point they glimpsed other beings who seemed to be "trapped" in an apparently most unfortunate state of existence. Those who described seeing these confused beings are in agreement on several points. First, they state that these beings seemed to be, in effect, unable to surrender their attachments to the physical world. One man recounted that the spirits he saw apparently "couldn't progress on the other side because their God is still living here." That is, they seemed bound to some particular object, person, or habit. Secondly, all have remarked that these beings appeared "dulled," that their consciousness seemed somehow limited in contrast with that of others. Thirdly, they say it appeared that these "dulled spirits" were to be there only until they solved whatever problem or difficulty was keeping them in that perplexed state.

These points of agreement come across in the

following segment of an interview with one woman who was believed "dead" for some fifteen minutes.

*You mentioned seeing these people—spirits who seemed very confused. Could you tell me more about them?*

These bewildered people? I don't know exactly where I saw them. . . . But as I was going by, there was this area that was dull—this is in contrast to all the brilliant light. The figures were more humanized than the rest of them were, if you stop to think of it in that respect, but neither were they in quite human form as we are.

What you would think of as their head was bent downward; they had sad, depressed looks; they seemed to shuffle, as someone would on a chain gang. I don't know why I say this because I don't remember noticing feet. I don't know what they were, but they looked washed out, dull, gray. And they seemed to be forever shuffling and moving around, not knowing where they were going, not knowing who to follow, or what to look for.

As I went by they didn't even raise their heads to see what was happening. They seemed to be thinking, "Well, it's all over with. What am I doing? What's it all about?" Just this absolute, crushed, hopeless demeanor—not knowing what to do or where to go or who they were or anything else.

They seemed to be forever moving, rather than just sitting, but in no special direction. They would start straight, then veer to the left and take a few steps and veer back to the right. And absolutely nothing to do. Searching, but for what they were searching I don't know.

*Did they seem to be aware of the physical world?*

They didn't seem to be aware of anything—not the physical world or the spiritual world. They seemed to be caught in between somewhere. It's neither spiritual nor physical. It's on a level somewhere between the two—or it appeared so to me. They may have some contact with the physical world. Something is tying them down, because they all seemed to be bent over and looking downward, maybe into the physical world . . . maybe watching something they hadn't done or should do. They couldn't make up their minds what to do, because they all had the most woebegone expressions; there was no color of life.

*So they seemed to be bewildered?*

Very bewildered; not knowing who they are or what they are. It looks like they have lost any knowledge of who they are, what they are—no identity whatsoever.

*Would you say they were in between the physical world and what you were in?*

In my memory, what I saw was after I left the physical hospital. As I said, I felt I rose upward and it was between, it was *before* I actually entered this tunnel—as I referred to it—and before I entered the spiritual world where there is so much brilliant sunlight—well, not sunlight, but the brilliant light that surrounded everything and was brighter than sunlight, but it didn't hurt like the sunlight can hurt your eyes, no glare to it. But in this particular place there was the dullest, drab gray. Now, I have a friend who is color blind and I've heard him say that the world to him is just shades and tones of gray. But to me, I'm full of color—and this was something that was maybe like a black and white movie. Just the different tones of gray—dingy, washed out.

They were not aware of me. They showed no sign of being aware that I was there. It was quite depressing.

They seemed to be trying to decide; they were looking back; they didn't know whether to go on or to return to the bodies where they were. They did seem to hover; they kept looking downward and never upward. They didn't want to go on to see what was awaiting them; they also reminded me of what I have read of as descriptions of ghosts; they would be mainly the see-through type of thing. There seems to have been a great huge array of them around.

Some persons who have seen this phenomenon have noticed certain of these beings apparently trying unsuccessfully to communicate with persons who were still physically alive. One man related many instances he observed while he was "dead" for an extended period of time. For example, he told how he saw an ordinary man walking, unaware, down the street while one of these dulled spirits hovered above him. He said he had the feeling that this spirit had been, while alive, the man's mother, and, still unable to give up her earthly role, was trying to tell her son what to do. The following excerpt from an interview with a woman subject relates another example.

*Could you see any of them trying to talk to other [physical] people?*

Un, huh. You could see them trying to make contact, but no one would realize that they were around; people would just ignore them. . . . They were trying to communicate, yet there was no way they could break through. People seemed to be completely unaware of them.

*Could you tell anything they were trying to say?*

One seemed to be a woman who was trying so hard to reach through to children and to an older woman in the house. I wondered if in some way this was the mother of the children, and maybe the daughter of the older woman in the house, and she was trying to break through to them. This seemed to me to be meaning that she was trying to reach the children and they continued to play and pay no attention, and the older person seemed to be going about in the kitchen doing work with no awareness that this person was around.

*Was there any particular thing she was trying to tell them?*

Well, it seems more or less that she was trying to get through to them, trying to tell them, seemingly, to do things differently from what they were doing now, to change, to make a change in their life style. Now, this sounds kind of put on, but she was trying to get them to do the right things, to change so as not to be left like she was. "Don't do as I did, so this won't happen to you. Do things for others so that you won't be left like this."

I'm not trying to moralize or make a sermon, but this seemed to be the message that she was trying to get across. . . . It seemed that in this house there was no love, if you want to put it that way. . . . It seemed that she was trying to atone for something she had done. . . . It's an experience I'll never forget.

# Supernatural Rescues

In several accounts I have collected, persons say that they had near-death experiences through which they were saved from physical death by the interposition of some spiritual agent or being. In each case, the person involved found himself (knowingly or unknowingly) in a potentially fatal accident or set of circumstances from which it was beyond his own powers to escape. He may even have given up and prepared himself to die. However, at this point a voice or a light manifested itself and rescued him from the brink of death. Persons undergoing this relate that afterward their lives were changed, that they came to feel they were saved from death for a purpose. They have all reported that their religious beliefs were strengthened.

One experience of this type which has become quite well known is that related in the book *A Man Called Peter*, by Catherine Marshall. She describes how, during his boyhood in Scotland, Peter Marshall was saved from falling to his death over a cliff in the fog by a voice which called to him from behind. This experience affected him greatly, and he went on to become a minister.

Here is a part of one interview in which a "rescue" of this type is reported. A man told me of being involved in an industrial accident in which he was trapped in a huge vat, into which a stream of very hot acid and steam was being pumped under high pressure. He recalled:

The heat of all this was terrific. I yelled, "Let me out of here. I'm getting trapped." I had gotten as far as I could into a corner, and put my face into the corner, but the stuff was so hot that it was burning me through my clothing. So, at that time I realized that in just a matter of minutes I would be scalded to death.

I guess it was in my weakness or whatever that I gave up. To myself, I just said, "This is it. I'm a goner." I could not see, and the heat was so intense that I could not open my eyes. I had my eyes closed the whole time. But it seemed that the whole area lit up with a glow. And a verse of Scripture that I had heard all my life, that had never meant too much to me, "Lo, I am with thee always," came from a direction which later turned out to be the only way out.

I couldn't stand to open my eyes, but I could still see that light, so I followed it. I know that my eyes were closed the whole time, though. The doctor didn't even treat my eyes later. No acid got in them. . . .

*Did this change your life in any way?*

After I got back to work, some of the people who work there were talking about how calm I was after the whole thing had happened. I'm not that brave a man; I don't have that much courage. The fact that I was led by an unseen hand out of the danger was the source of my courage, was the calmness they saw. It was not in me. The voice that led me out was the same voice that gave me that courage.

I know that the hand of Jesus Christ reached down and got me out of that place. I think it's not a matter of think, it's a matter of *know* that it was God's will that my life be spared—for what reason, I don't know. At that time I was not living as close to God as I should have. I have been drawn closer to him by this. I still have problems. I know that a God that can step in and save a man in a moment of crisis can handle anything. So I have learned to depend on him.

*When you heard the voice, was it just like a normal physical voice?*

No. It was as if it was magnified, amplified. There was no question that I heard. There was no question as to the direction it came from. If it had come from my right or from my left, and I had followed it, I would have been instantly killed. The fact that it came from the direction it came from and that I followed the voice was why I came out alive. . . . Never would I have stepped out into that heat myself. I knew what I was in for.

[This voice] was a commanding voice—not "Will you come this way?" The first thing that popped into my mind was "Here I am down here by myself and I'm going to die." And when I heard that voice, there was no doubt in my mind, I knew that within myself I had no way to get out.

*How long did this last?*

It seemed like an eternity. In other words if you are crawling some forty or fifty feet through acid, each time you make a move you know you are moving at top speed. I would say the whole thing happened in a matter of a couple or three minutes after I saw that I was trapped, but it seemed like an eternity.

*Did this seem like a normal physical light?*

No. It was nothing like I had ever seen before. It was what you might see if you looked up into the sunlight. And this was a dark place where I was trapped. It was a big bright light and a voice. I didn't see a figure or anything like that. I followed the light the whole way.

*Did the light seem to hurt your eyes? Was it uncomfortable to look into it?*

No. Not in any way.

*Did it seem to have any particular color?*

No. Nothing other than just a bright white light. It was like the sun—like looking into the sun.

Another man reported:

This was during World War II . . . and I was serving in the infantry in Europe. I had an experience I won't ever forget. . . . I saw an enemy plane diving toward the building we were in, and it had opened fire on us. . . . The dust from the bullets was headed in a path right toward us. I was very scared and thought we would all be killed.

I didn't see a thing, but I felt a wonderful, comforting presence there with me, and a kind, gentle voice said, "I'm here with you, Reid. Your time has not come yet." I was so relaxed and comfortable in that presence. . . . Since that day, I have not been one bit afraid of death.

Finally, here is the account of one woman who was extremely ill with an infection. Note that in this example the patient seems to have been instructed and guided in her own resuscitation.

> The doctors had all given up on me. They said I was dying. . . . I got to the point where I was feeling the life going out of my body. . . . I could still hear what everyone was saying, though I couldn't see anything. I wished I could live to raise my children and to play a part in their lives. . . .
>
> That's when I heard God's voice talking to me. He had the most loving gentle voice. . . . I know I wasn't out of my head, as some people might think. . . . I could hear the voices of the others in the room, in the background . . . but I could sense his voice, too, and it was so overwhelming. He told me that if I wanted to live, I was going to have to breathe . . . and so I did, and when I took that one breath, I started to come back. Then he told me to breathe again, and I was able to take another breath, and life came back into my body. . . .
>
> The doctors were amazed. They had all given me up, and naturally they hadn't heard the voice I had. They couldn't understand what happened.

I will close this chapter by reminding the reader that these are by no means common accounts of near-death experiences. However, they have occurred in a sizable number of my cases and each of them is connected, within the context of the particular experience, with the elements which were reported earlier. For example, in the first interview quoted under "The Vision of Knowledge" above, the subject also described being out of her body, going through a dark tunnel, seeing the events of her life in review, and many other of the common elements. Similarly, note that the passage through a dark tunnel and being out of the body are prominently reported in two of the interviews quoted above in "Cities of Light." In each case, these new features—like the ones with which I have previously dealt—were described to me by ordinary people, who were not seeking these experiences, who had no previous interest in or knowledge of such matters, and yet who, afterward, had absolutely no doubt about the reality of what they had seen.

¹ Edith Hamilton and Huntington Cairns, eds., *The Collected Dialogues of Plato*, trans. Hugh Tredennick, Bollingen Series 71 (New York: Pantheon Books, 1961), p. 844.

# 2
# JUDGMENT

I n discussing *Life After Life*, one reviewer stated:

> The area sure to provoke controversy among religious groups is a section dealing with models of the afterlife. Most of the individuals interviewed did not experience any reward-punishment crisis—the traditional model of being reviewed by a St. Peter type before being admitted to the afterlife.[1]

Many people have brought up this point, so it seems appropriate to examine something in near-death experiences which may or may not, according to one's theology, be likened to the concept of a judgment. Again and again, my near-death subjects have described to me a panoramic, wrap-around, full-color, three-dimensional vision of the events of their lives. Some people say that during this vision they saw only the major events of their lives. Others go so far as to say that in the course of this panorama every single thing that they had ever done or thought was there for them to see. All the good things and all the bad were portrayed there at once, instantaneously. It will be remembered also that this panorama was quite frequently said to have taken place in the presence of a "being of light," whom some Christians identified as Christ, and that this being asked them a question, in effect, "What have you done with your life?"

In being pressed to explain as precisely as they can what the point of this question was, most people come up with something like the formulation of one man who put it to me most succinctly when he said that he was asked whether he had done the things he did *because* he loved others, that is, from the *motivation* of love. At this point, one might say, a kind of judgment took place, for in this state of heightened awareness, when people saw any selfish acts which they had done they felt extremely repentant. Likewise, when gazing upon those events in which they had shown love and kindness they felt satisfaction.

It is interesting to note that the judgment in the cases I studied came not from the being of light, who seemed to love and accept these people anyway, but rather from within the individual being judged. A passage in Matthew respecting judgment is of some significance in this regard. The King James Version of *The Bible* has the passage translated as follows (Matthew 7:1-2):

> Judge not, that ye be not judged. For with what judgment ye judge, ye shall be judged; and with what measure ye mete, it shall be measured to you again.

However, in *Today's English Version of the New Testament* (also published as *Good News for Modern Man*), the following translation is given:

Do not judge others, so that God will not judge you—because God will judge you in the same way you judge others, and he will apply to you the same rules you apply to others.

I am not a Biblical scholar, so I cannot rule on which of these translations is the more accurate. However, I find it very interesting that, purely from the point of view of what my near-death subjects reported experiencing, the first translation would be more applicable—the judgment came from within them. In this state, they seemed to have seen for themselves what they should and shouldn't have done and to have judged themselves accordingly.

In thinking about all this, it has occurred to me that a very common theme of near-death experiences is the feeling of being *exposed* in one way or another. From one point of view we human beings can be characterized as creatures who spend a great deal of our time hiding behind various masks. We seek inner security through money or power; we try to make ourselves feel that we are better than others by priding ourselves on our social class, the degree of our education, the color of our skin, our money, our power, the beauty of our bodies, our identification with a male or female role, etc. We adorn our bodies with clothes; we hide our innermost thoughts and certain of our deeds from the knowledge or sight of others.

However, in the moments around the time of death all such masks are necessarily dropped. Suddenly, the person finds his every thought and deed portrayed in a three-dimensional, full-color panorama. If he meets other beings he reports that they know his every thought and vice versa. He finds that in this state communication is not mediated through words, but rather that thoughts are understood directly—to the point where, as one man put it, "You're too embarrassed to be around people who don't think the way you do."

The beauty of the physical body or the color of the skin can no longer be a source of pride. Indeed, people do not have physical bodies any more. The only beauty which appears now has nothing at all to do with the body; it is whatever beauty there may be in the soul. Sexual identity is dropped too; most people feel that they had no specific male or female identity while in this state. It is somehow natural, then, that in these final moments two qualities which distinctly pertain to the mind, namely love and knowledge, stand forth in prominent relief.

One other feature of this review which might be mentioned is that some report that in addition to their acts, they can see portrayed before them the consequences of their acts for others. As one man put it most graphically:

> I first was out of my body, above the building, and I could see my body lying there. Then I became aware of the light—just light—being all around me. Then it seemed there was a display all around me, and everything in my life just

went by for review, you might say. I was really very, very ashamed of a lot of the things that I experienced because it seemed that I had a different knowledge, that the light was showing me what was wrong, what I did wrong. And it was very real.

It seemed like this flashback, or memory, or whatever was directed primarily at ascertaining the extent of my life. It was like there was a judgment being made and then, all of a sudden, the light became dimmer, and there was a conversation, not in words, but in thoughts. When I would see something, when I would experience a past event, it was like I was seeing it through eyes with (I guess you would say) omnipotent knowledge, guiding me, and helping me to see.

That's the part that has stuck with me, because it showed me not only what I had done but *even how what I had done had affected other people.* And it wasn't like I was looking at a movie projector because I could *feel* these things; there was feeling, and particularly since I was with this knowledge . . . I found out that not even your thoughts are lost. . . . Every thought was there. . . . Your thoughts are not lost. . . .

This situation can be regarded as being most unpleasant indeed, and it is no wonder that quite frequently people may come back from this feeling that they need to make a change in their lives. Consider the following passages taken from interviews with two men.

(1) I didn't tell anybody about my experience, but when I got back, I had this overwhelming, burning, consuming desire to do something for other people. . . . I was so ashamed of all the

things that I had done, or hadn't done, in my life. I felt like I had to do it, that it couldn't wait.

(2) When I got back from this, I had decided I'd better change. I was very repentant. I hadn't been satisfied with the life I had led up to then, so I wanted to start doing better.

Although many people continue to ask me whether anyone with whom I have talked has reported a hell, it remains true that in the mass of material I have collected no one has ever described to me a state like the archetypical hell. However, I might remark that I have never interviewed anyone who had been a real rounder prior to his close call. The people I have interviewed have been normal, nice people. Such transgressions as they were guilty of had been minor—the sorts of things we have all done. So one would not expect that they would have been consigned to a fiery pit. Yet nothing I have encountered precludes the possibility of a hell.

Some people seem to be bothered by the fact that the being of light is reported in these near-death experiences to be so totally loving and forgiving and to love people despite their many shortcomings, which are there revealed so graphically before him. For my own part, I can only say that I love my children despite their faults and that I am certain I would continue to love them no matter what they might do.

Others seem dissatisfied because they apparently think that these experiences are inconsistent with the notion of a Final Judgment at the end of the world. I see no discrepancy here. Obviously, if anyone were to have come back from "death" reporting that he went through the Final Judgment, then his experience would have been mistaken. Since the end of the world has not yet taken place, any report of its having occurred during a near-death experience would be, in effect, a disconfirmation of the validity of that experience. There may well be a Final Judgment; near-death experiences in no way imply the contrary. Indeed, many of the persons whom I have interviewed have mentioned their belief that this will take place. It should be added, though, that they accept this on the basis of scriptural authority alone and did not derive it from anything they learned or foresaw while in their state of near or apparent "death."

Notions of heaven and hell, judgment, the Final Judgment, the end of the world, and God's grace are all eschatological concepts which form the basis for much debate among theologians. They are all so ultimate, so cosmic in their importance that it is very hard for us human beings to talk about them directly, in mere human language. Hence, they have sometimes been portrayed in more picturesque, figurative terms.

As one goes through the history of painting in Europe, the concept of the judgment is portrayed at various ages through the use of such symbols as a record book or an account book, a court of law, and scales (the weighing out of souls). Plato, in his myth of Er, talks about the "markers" that souls which are facing judgment wear. In the *Tibetan Book of the Dead* the concept is portrayed as a "mirror of Karma." Remember that all along my near-death subjects have told me that the words they use to describe their experiences are only analogies or metaphors used to indicate experiences which ultimately lie beyond all human language. It is somehow not surprising, then, that the particular words used in our technological age are drawn from such contexts as the science of optics, as when the word "images" was used, or from technological developments such as slides or movies, and that these days the symbolism used almost reminds one of some of the more fantastic developments in the science of photography or in television technology; of the three-dimensional hologram or of the instant replay.

One final remark, with respect to the question of what might happen to persons such as the perpetrators of the Nazi horrors. If what my subjects have reported happens to everybody, imagine for a moment what would happen to them during this review, especially if, as some say, they see not only their selfish acts but also the consequences of those acts for others. Those who engineered the Nazi atrocities seem to have been people whose lack of love was so complete that they willed the deaths of millions of innocent persons. This resulted in countless individual tragedies of separation of parent from child, of husband from wife, of friend from friend. It resulted in innumerable long, lingering deaths and fast brutal ones. It resulted in awful degradations, in years of hunger, tears, and torment for their victims. If what happened to my subjects happened to these men, they would see all these things and many others come alive, vividly portrayed before them. In my wildest fantasies, I am totally unable to imagine a hell more horrible, more ultimately unbearable than this.

[1] Frederic A. Brussat, review of *Life After Life* in *Cultural Information Service*, Nov. 1976, pp. 16–17.

# 3
## SUICIDE

The term "suicide" is used in connection with a wide variety of at least potentially self-destructive behaviors which stem from many different apparent motives or conditions and which manifest themselves under widely varying circumstances. For many centuries mankind has been grappling with the many implications of suicidal behavior. At first it was approached from the theological, ethical, and philosophical points of view. In more recent times sociological and psychological perspectives have been added. Despite this long probing, many puzzling questions remain.

Given the fact that some people who have been revived from very close encounters with death have reported spiritual experiences, some have asked how these reports bear on the issue of suicide. The first thing that one must point out is that consideration of near-death experiences does not give us final answers to the many different kinds of puzzles we have about suicide. All we can do is address ourselves to two questions. First: Do persons who have had near-death experiences from causes other than suicidal attempts come back with any particular attitude toward suicide? And second: Do reported near-death experiences which resulted from suicidal attempts differ in any way from those which had other causes?

While people who have reported near-death experiences state quite often that they felt they did not want to come back from "death," nonetheless they all disavow suicide as a means of returning to this state. They come back saying that they feel they have learned in the course of their experience that they have a purpose to fulfill here in life. They return with a serious, dedicated attitude toward life and living. Absolutely no one that I have interviewed has sought a repeat performance of their experience.

Numerous people who had "died" of natural or accidental causes have told me that while they were in this state, it had been intimated to them that suicide was a very unfortunate act which was attended with a penalty. For example, one man who "died" after an accident told me:

> [While I was over there] I got the feeling that two things it would be completely forbidden for me to do would be to kill myself or to kill another person. . . . If I were to commit suicide I would be throwing God's gift back in his face. . . . Killing somebody else would be interfering with God's purpose for that individual.

Another man who survived an apparent clinical death of some duration said that while he was "over there" he had the impression that there was a "penalty" to pay for some acts of suicide, and that part of this would be to witness the suffering on the part of others that this act would cause.

At the time I completed the manuscript of my first book I had encountered very few significant cases of near-death resulting from attempted suicide. I think this is understandable in that persons who have had such experiences might be more reluctant to talk about them because of possible residual guilt feelings about the attempt. Since that time, however, I have come upon some additional cases. All of these people agree on one point: they felt their suicidal attempts solved nothing. They found that they were involved in exactly the same problems from which they had been trying to extricate themselves by suicide. Whatever difficulty they had been trying to get away from was still there on the other side, unresolved.

One person mentioned being "trapped" in the situation which had provoked her suicide attempt. She had the feeling that the state of affairs in which she had been before her "death" was being repeated again and again, as if in a cycle.

This problem I was telling you about, you know, well, looking back on it now, of course, it doesn't seem so important, from a more adult way of looking at it. But at the time, as I was a person at that age, it really seemed very important. . . . Well, the thing was, it was still around, even when I was "dead." And it was like it was repeating itself, a rerun. I would go through it once and at the end I would think, "Oh, I'm glad that's over," and then it would start all over again, and I would think, "Oh, no, not this again."

All mentioned that after their experiences, they would never consider trying suicide again. Their common attitude is that they had made a mistake, and that they were very glad they had not succeeded in their attempts. For instance, when I asked one man whether, in the light of what he had experienced, he would ever again choose to try to kill himself, he answered:

> No. I would not do that again. I will die naturally next time, because one thing I realized at that time is that our life here is just such a small period of time and there is so much which needs to be done while you're here. And, when you die it's eternity.

It is quite interesting that the views and experiences outlined above coincide so closely with the sentiments expressed in a certain very ancient theological argument against suicide. Many diverse theologians and philosophers over the ages have argued against suicide from the premise that we are in life, in effect, on assignment or "as a gift" from God, and that it is just not our option to take our own lives. Thus Plato, in the *Phaedo*, alludes to the doctrine that we are placed on earth in a sort of post, and that we must not run away from it. He argues that, in essence, we belong to and are in the care of God and must not try to release ourselves in this way.[1] In the Middle Ages, Thomas Aquinas propounded the argument that since life is a kind of gift from God to man, it is up to God alone to make the judgment as to when it should end.[2] John Locke, the seventeenth-century British philosopher to whom we owe some of the ideas in the Declaration of Independence and the Constitution, declared, too, that we are the property of God and are placed here on his business, not to quit our stations willfully.[3]

Likewise, the German philosopher Immanuel Kant, a very different thinker indeed from the others, wrote:

> . . . as soon as we examine suicide from the standpoint of religion we immediately see it in its true light. We have been placed in this world under certain conditions and for specific purposes. But a suicide opposes the purpose of his creator; he arrives in the other world as one who has deserted his post; he must be looked upon as a rebel against God. . . . God is our owner; we are his property; his providence works for our good.[4]

I do not present the above arguments to endorse their reasoning or to make an ethical or moral judgment about suicide. My only point is to suggest that much the same feelings about man's purpose in life and how that relates to the problem of suicide are expressed both in these theological arguments and in the words and thoughts of people who have had near-death experiences.

I realize that the experiences I have quoted in this chapter raise many questions. Some have pointed out that in certain cultures suicide is not morally condemned, as it generally is in our own. It may even be regarded as an honorable act, as in the case of Japan during the age of the samurai. One may ask, "Would a person from such a society report the same kind of experiences upon resuscitation from a suicidal 'death'?"

Further, some have suggested that, in effect, we are all committing suicide in one way or another. That is, most of us probably engage in some sort of activity which—we should know—will eventually harm us or cause our deaths. Three examples which are striking in our own society are smoking cigarettes, eating foods which have high levels of cholesterol, and driving under the influence of alcohol. People go right on doing these things despite their full knowledge that these actions could eventually result in death from any one of several diseases or from an automobile wreck. What is the difference, one might ask, between such behavior and "real" suicide? At what point on the spectrum of potentially self-destructive behavior would the "penalties" mentioned by the subjects quoted above begin to take effect?

Some persons commit suicide for altruistic reasons, to save others, for example. What would people who undergo such "heroic" deaths experience? Or what of persons who take their own lives in the throes of psychotic depression or horrendous loss?

It is also a well known fact that many who "attempt" suicide do not really intend to kill themselves, but are merely trying to draw the attention of others to their needs or problems in a dramatic way. Conversely, many psychiatrists hold that so-called accident-prone individuals, while they have no conscious desire to kill themselves, nonetheless *subconsciously* wish to do so. In this explanation, their apparent accidents would be unconscious suicidal attempts.

Obviously, no one has the final answers to such complex questions, and I am not trying to over-simplify these issues. All I can do is to report that the near-death experiences of which I am aware that took place in association with attempted suicides were different from others in the ways described.

When asked about such matters, a psychiatrist friend of mine, who had an "other-world" experience during an apparent clinical death from an infection, gave an interesting answer. He expressed the belief that God, in his nature, is much more forgiving, understanding, and just than we as humans are able to comprehend, and that God will take care of these things in accordance with his love and wisdom. What a suicidal person needs from us as fellow humans is not judgment but love and understanding.

[1] Plato, *Phaedo*, 61.

[2] Thomas Aquinas, *Summa Theologica*, Part II-II, Question 64, Article 5.

[3] John Locke, *The Second Treatise on Civil Government*, Section 6.

[4] Immanuel Kant, *Lectures on Ethics*, trans. Louise Infield (New York: Harper & Row, 1963), Harper Torchbook ed., pp. 153–154.

# 4

# REACTIONS
# FROM THE MINISTRY

In her foreword to *Life After Life*, Dr. Elisabeth Kubler-Ross predicted that this type of study would receive criticism from some members of the clergy. To a certain extent this has been true. However, many Christian ministers of various denominations have told me of their enthusiasm and interest in this kind of study and have invited me to speak on the subject to their congregations.

Numerous ministers have told me that they have had parishioners who told them of near-death experiences; they seemed pleased to get the insight of someone whose professional background lies outside the ministry. Quite a few ministers have told me that they feel these experiences confirm things which are said about life after death in *The Bible*. *Guideposts* magazine, which is decidedly Christian in its orientation and outlook, has been publishing accounts such as these for years.

One Methodist minister who had been investigating near-death experiences himself before our paths crossed told me of something that took place after he and I began doing some research together.

The following is an excerpt from a dialogue between us about the significance of what we had been doing.

MINISTER: This lady was terminally ill. She had kidney disease. And in talking with her about death before she died, I had affirmed my belief in life after death. I told her that one of the things that had strengthened my faith was the kind of research that had been done by medical doctors in terms of interviewing people who had died and been resuscitated. I had told her about this and it excited her. She brought the thing back up in subsequent visits.

At her funeral, when I delivered the eulogy I mentioned the talks I had with her about this, and how this had tended to affirm her faith. The real thing about this was the way it affected the people in the pews, for me as a clergyman to affirm the fact that I believed that [this lady] was still alive and the fact that a physician friend of mine believes that, too. She had been very close to her husband, and it was like a part of her had died when he died several years before. And I said in that sermon that she had gone to be with him, in some place with Christ. And I wasn't speaking figuratively or symbolically; I meant it. This gave them comfort. . . .

After that funeral an unusual thing happened. People always come up to you after preaching a sermon on Sunday and tell you that you did well, but never after a funeral. It's unheard of. Yet, about ten people afterward came up and complimented me on what I said at that funeral. . . .

One of the things I'm trying to do in preaching is to lead people to love. And if I tell them that at the time of death, Christ comes to people and asks them, "How have you loved?"; that love seems to be a thing Christ points out, not only in *The Bible* back there two thousand years ago but in the now, as people experience death and experience this positive sense of judgment, this affirms faith. This is a tool that I've used several times in preaching to reinforce faith, to lead people to see the importance of faith and love.

DR. MOODY: *You mentioned earlier that like me, you think that a proof of life after death, in the sense of a scientific proof, is not likely to come.*

MINISTER: Well, if we could prove life after death, which would be similar to proving the existence of God, then that would invalidate the system of faith. We cannot prove any of the ultimate things in life. The highest life has to be accepted by faith, and if we were able to short-circuit that and prove that life does exist beyond the grave, people wouldn't have to have any faith in order to believe. Life is a mystery. Life after death is a mystery.

And if we could ever break down the code, then we wouldn't need to operate on faith and this would short-circuit the whole system. So it ultimately must be accepted on faith. But what people who come back from death say does give some affirmation of faith and reinforces it. It affirms my faith, for I am already a man of faith. But if I were not a man of faith, this would not convince me.

That was the opinion of one Methodist minister, but I would not have expected to have every member of the ministry agree. A few ministers have come up with specific objections. One kind of objection has come from some theologically liberal ministers who see the function of the church as essentially an ethical task, having to do with advancing social reform and helping to establish social justice for all. From this theological perspective, they seem to have come to the conclusion that concern with survival of bodily death is old-fashioned. I have heard several such ministers remark that they feel that the concern with life after death is vanishing, or at least that it should be.

In keeping with this viewpoint, an elderly Episcopalian minister recently asked me, in effect, "Shouldn't you think about *this* world, and not the next? Aren't there a lot of problems to be solved *here?*" He went on to say that often in the past, leaders have tried to distract the attention of disadvantaged peoples or other victims of social injustice from their earthly plight by promising that things will be better for them in heaven if they don't get out of line or rock the boat by disobeying the rules. In other words, his antagonism toward the study of near-death phenomena seemed to be based on the concept that doctrines of the afterlife have sometimes represented disguised attempts at social suppression.

To a certain extent I am in agreement with some of the sentiments expressed by these representatives of the ministry. My own feeling is that—yes—there are many real social injustices in this world, and I personally would like, in the course of my own life, to help correct these things. I do feel that the commandment to "love thy neighbor as thyself" is important, and this implies that we should do everything we can to help improve the lot of our fellow man; to help those less fortunate than ourselves.

And yet, there are several points at which my perspective and experience differ from those which these ministers apparently have had. In the light of my own experience, I am surprised to find that some ministers feel that concern over the issue of whether there is personal survival of bodily death is on the wane or is vanishing. My own observation differs sharply. I feel that indeed many people *are* still greatly interested in this issue. Also, I find that I am unable to see how social concern and interest in life after death are mutually exclusive. Surely, one could go on being concerned about the welfare of others even if he were to have full awareness of the fact that there is life after death and an interest in any findings relating to this possibility. In fact, many of the subjects with whom I have talked have expressed intense concern for the welfare of others. They came back from their experiences feeling challenged to live and to get things done for others while here on earth. I personally share these aims. After all, rather than making us indifferent to social injustice, belief in an afterlife may give us an incentive to try to correct it.

Further, I cannot agree that the only—or even a primary—factor in the persistence of doctrines of life after death is to distract people from their unsatisfactory existence. Many persons have told me of their fears of death; they don't like to think that their consciousness may be obliterated at death. Others miss friends and relatives they have lost through death and hope that those persons still live somewhere. These concerns seem far removed from matters of social injustice or class suppression.

In addition, my own approach to these experiences has been shaped by my medical interests. Persons have told me—as a physician—about experiences of theirs which were very significant in their lives and which came about in connection with their contact with medical resuscitation measures. As such, I think that this is a medical issue, too. As far as I can, I would like to be able to understand experiences which are very important to my patients and which tend to happen to them in situations in which they are under medical care.

I am not trying to say here that my perspective is any better than that of the liberal ministers I mentioned, only that it is *different*. Thus, it could be that their feeling that concern about life after death is fading is a projection of their own limited association with like-minded ministers or with their own socially concerned parishioners. Similarly, however, it could be that my own feeling that concern with this issue is still rampant is a projection of my own limited experience, mainly with many people who did express an interest in this. I don't at all claim to know where the majority of Christian opinion on this issue lies.

The second group of ministers who have voiced criticism of near-death experiences speak from a theological perspective which lies on the conservative side of the spectrum. I am referring to those who say that near-death experiences are directed by satanic forces or evil demons.

I do not have any formal training in the field of theology. My reading in it is largely limited to the works of the great theologians, such as St. Augustine, Thomas Aquinas, and John Calvin, who are also considered great and influential philosophers. But I have asked friends who are ministers and theologians what they think about such charges. The consensus of what they have told me is that a vision is to be counted as valid if, among other things, the effects it has on a person's life are of a certain kind: if it makes him feel closer to God, for example, or it leads him to want to follow religious teachings. As we have seen earlier, the near-death experiences of the persons I have interviewed have led them in precisely these ways. Other ministers have also cited the criterion that such visions must be consistent with what is stated in *The Bible* and have shared with me their feeling that this criterion is satisfied in this case.

For my part, I must confess that it was unsettling to be accused—even if only by implication—of being in league with the devil. My religious belief is very important to me, and one hardly knows how to defend oneself against such an accusation as Satanism. I felt somewhat relieved, however, after talking with a Methodist minister who is of a most conservative and fundamentalist temperament. He assured me that he, too, had been accused by members of a sect which is slightly more conservative than his own of being one of Satan's helpers. I daresay I must content myself with the reflection that in this huge, diverse world there will always be those who impugn one's motivation. I can but hope that, in the respects in which I am in the wrong, someone will come along to help lead me back onto the correct path.

There is a third group of ministers who should be mentioned in connection with this discussion. They have expressed what is not so much criticism as a kind of timidity. They seem to feel inadequate to comment on these experiences because they think of them as lying more in the realm of medicine: a phenomenon which ought to be left to the patient's doctor. They may, for example, discount such experiences by saying that they were merely hallucinations. This is despite the fact that the persons having these experiences relate them to their religious lives and beliefs rather than to their health.

This is yet another manifestation of an old dilemma—the conflict between professions. All professions seem to have certain members who jealously guard their own territory from intrusions by others. Such persons are resentful when an informed layman or a person from another field of study comments on some item relating to their own professional domain. Also, all professions have some members who are reluctant to show interest in or concern for issues that lie outside their personal province or specialty.

It is desirable to be on guard against oversimplification of complex problems, but there are difficulties inherent in this kind of professional exclusivism. This attitude seems to be most stifling intellectually. It is also more likely to shut out any insight which might be contributed to a profession's understanding of its subject matter by outsiders.

In addition, this attitude seems to involve the highly dubious assumption that the present division of labor among professions and fields of study exhausts all reality. I should think that from the point of view of an issue or of a new phenomenon, it must be a horrible fate indeed to be caught in the borderline between the provinces of two human professions.

To relate all of this to the topic at hand, I have met ministers who seem reluctant to talk about anything which appears in any way medical. I have had occasion to meet the ministers of quite a few of my patients, and I was surprised at the apologetic manner some of them displayed when discussing the medical aspects of these cases, especially since they showed a most impressive degree of understanding of the patient's condition and prognosis. So, I have found ministers who will not discuss near-death experiences because they feel that they represent medical phenomena. On the other hand, several physicians have told me that they would not discuss such experiences with their patients because they feel that they are within the realm of the patient's religious life. In short, it appears that to some people this phenomenon is one of those areas lying between two worlds which is predestined to be unpopular.

On the whole I have been pleased that most of the ministers whom I already knew or have met in the course of doing this study have been interested in and have expressed approval of my work. They also realize that I do not draw conclusions, that I am not trying to force my own personal feelings on others and that, being fully aware of my own limitations, I welcome comment and guidance from other perspectives.

# 5

# HISTORICAL
# EXAMPLES

Several years ago, when I was asked whether I knew of any historical examples of the near-death phenomenon, I had to answer in the negative. Since then it has become obvious that there is a wealth of accounts of near-death experiences available in writings from earlier times. I think it would be worthwhile to quote here at length from various sources, drawn from different cultures and ages. What follows is only a fraction of the material I have gathered to date, and what I have already gathered is probably only the tip of the iceberg.

The story of the stoning of the apostle Stephen has been pointed out as a possible near-death experience. In Acts 7:54–58, it is related that just before Stephen was stoned to death by an aroused mob (and apparently before any actual injury took place), he had a vision:

> When they heard these things, they were cut to the heart, and they gnashed on him with their teeth. But he, being full of the Holy Ghost, looked up steadfastly into heaven, and saw the glory of God, and Jesus standing on the right

hand of God. And said, Behold, I see the heavens
opened, and the Son of man standing on the
right hand of God. Then they cried out with a
loud voice, and stopped their ears, and ran upon
him with one accord, and cast him out of the
city, and stoned him: and the witnesses laid
down their clothes at a young man's feet, whose
name was Saul.

The Venerable Bede was an English monk who
lived from 673 to 735 A.D. He completed *A History of the English Church and People* in 731 A.D.
Among many wonders, Bede relates a "return from
the dead" story which, allowing for differences in
cultural idiom, resembles in many respects those
heard today.

About this time, a noteworthy miracle, like
those of olden days, occurred in Britain. For, in
order to arouse the living from spiritual death,
a man already dead returned to bodily life and
related many notable things that he had seen,
some of which I have thought it valuable to
mention here in brief. There was a head of a
family living in a place in the country of the
Northumbrians known as Cunningham, who led
a devout life with all his household. He fell ill
and grew steadily worse until the crisis came, and
in the early hours of one night he died. But at
daybreak he returned to life and suddenly sat
up to the great consternation of those weeping
around the body, who ran away; only his wife,
who loved him more dearly, remained with him,
though trembling and fearful. The man reassured
her and said: "Do not be frightened; for I have
truly risen from the grasp of death, and I am
allowed to live among men again. But hence-
forward I must not live as I used to, and must

adopt a very different way of life." . . . Not long afterward, he abandoned all worldly responsibilities and entered the monastery of Melrose, which is almost completely surrounded by a bend in the river Tweed. . . .

This was the account he used to give of his experience: "A handsome man in a shining robe was my guide, and we walked in silence in what appeared to be a northeasterly direction. As we traveled onward, we came to a very broad and deep valley of infinite length. . . . He soon brought me out of darkness into an atmosphere of clear light, and as he led me forward in bright light, I saw before us a tremendous wall which seemed to be of infinite length and height in all directions. As I could see no gate, window, or entrance in it, I began to wonder why we went up to the wall. But when we reached it, all at once—I know not by what means—we were on top of it. Within lay a very broad and pleasant meadow. . . . Such was the light flooding all this place that it seemed greater than the brightness of daylight or of the sun's rays at noon. . . .

[The guide said,] " 'You must now return to your body and live among men once more; but, if you will weigh your actions with greater care and study to keep your words and ways virtuous and simple, then when you die you too will win a home among these happy spirits that you see. For, when I left you for a while, I did so in order to discover what your future would be.' When he told me this, I was most reluctant to return to my body; for I was entranced by the pleasantness and beauty of the place I could see and the company that I saw there. But I did not dare to question my guide, and meanwhile, I know not how, I suddenly found myself alive among men once more."

This man of God would not discuss these and

other things that he had seen with any apathetic
or careless-living people, but only with those
who were haunted by fear of punishment or
gladdened by the hope of eternal joys, and were
willing to take his words to heart and grow in
holiness.[1]

Features of particular interest in the above nar-
ration include the striking way in which the man's
life and outlook were changed by his experience,
the presence of a spirit who was there to guide
him through the transition, and his reluctance to
tell this to anyone who would not listen open-
mindedly and sympathetically.

Two interesting stories by unknown Irish au-
thors (from the tenth and ninth centuries respec-
tively) appear in an excellent collection of Celtic
literature, *A Celtic Miscellany*, translated by Kenneth H. Jackson.

### The Little Boys Who Went to Heaven

. . . Donnán son of Liath, one of Senán's
disciples, went to gather dulse on the shore,
with two little boys who were studying along
with him. The sea carried off his boat from him,
so that he had no boat to fetch the boys, and
there was no other boat on the island to rescue
the boys. So the boys were drowned on a rock;
but on the next day their bodies were carried so
that they lay on the beach of the island. The
parents came then and stood on the beach, and
asked that their sons should be given them alive.
Senán said to Donnán, "Tell the boys to arise
and speak with me." Donnán said to the boys,
"You may arise to talk with your parents, for
Senán tells you to do so." They arose at once at

Senán's command, and said to their parents, "You have done wrong to us, bringing us away from the land to which we came." "How could you prefer," said their mother to them, "to stay in that land rather than to come to us?" "Mother," they said, "though you should give us power over the whole world, and all its enjoyment and delight, we should think it no different from being in prison, compared with being in the life and in the world to which we came. Do not delay us, for it is time for us to go back again to the land from which we have come; and God shall bring it about for our sake that you shall not mourn after us." So their parents gave them their consent, and they went together with Senán to his oratory; and the sacrament was given them, and they went to heaven, and their bodies were buried in front of the oratory where Senán lived. And these were the first dead who were buried in Scattery Island.

## A Ghost Story

There were two students who were studying together, so that they were foster-brothers since they were small children. This was their talk, in their little hut: "It is a sad journey on which our dear ones and our friends go from us, that they never come back again with news for us of the land to which they go. Let us make a plan, that whoever of us dies first should come with news to the other." "Let it be done, truly." They undertook that whoever of them should die first should come before the end of a month with news to the other.

Not long after this, then, one of the two died. He was buried by the other, and he sang his requiem. He was expecting him until the end of a month, but the other did not come; and he

was abusing him and abusing the Trinity, so that
the soul begged the Trinity to let it go to talk
with him. Now, the latter was making prostra-
tions in his hut, and there was a little lintel above
his head; his head struck against the lintel so that
he fell lifeless. His soul saw the body lying before
it, but it thought it was still in its body. It was
looking at it. "But this is bad," it said, "to bring
me a dead body. It is the brotherhood of the
church, truly," it said, "who have brought it."
At that it bounded out of the house. One of the
clergy was ringing the bell. "It is not right,
priest," it said, "to bring the dead body to me."
The priest did not answer. It betook itself to
everyone. They did not hear. It was greatly
distressed. It betook itself out of the church to
the reapers. "Here I am," it said. They did not
hear. Fury seized it. It went to its church again.
They had gone to take tithes to him, and his body
was seen in the house, and it was brought to the
graveyard.

When the soul went into the church, it saw
its friend before it. "Well now," it said, "you have
been a long time coming; yours was a bad
promise." "Do not reproach me," said the other,
"I have come many a time, and would be beside
your pillow pleading with you, and you did not
hear; for the dense heavy body does not hear the
light ethereal tenuous soul." "I hear you now,"
it said. "No," said the other, "it is your soul only
that is here. It is from your own body that you
are escaping. For you have begged me to meet
you, and that has come about, then. Woe is him
who does wrong! Happy is he who does right!
Go to find your body before it is put into the
grave." "I will never go into it again, for horror
and fear of it!" "You shall go; you shall be alive
for a year. Recite the *Beati* every day for my
soul, for the *Beati* is the strongest ladder and

chain and collar to bring a man's soul out of hell."

It said farewell to the other, and went to its
body, and as it went into it it gave a shriek, and
came back to life; and went to heaven at the end
of a year. So the *Beati* is the best prayer there is.[2]

In these two accounts there are features found
in many contemporary experiences. In both of
these stories we have the now familiar "reluctance
to return." In the second there is the feeling that
the spirit has departed the body. The student
views his body, which he fails at first to recognize
as his own (a remark which several persons have
made to me in describing their experiences). He
notices the "one-way mirror" effect; that is, although he is able to hear and see others, he is
apparently invisible and inaudible to them. Also,
he is greeted by his departed friend.

An interesting account from another culture is
given in a book by Sir Edward Burnett Tylor, a
nineteenth-century English anthropologist. In
*Primitive Culture*, he quotes the following Poly-
nesian story.

This story . . . was told to Mr. Shortland by a
servant of his named Te Wharewera. An aunt of
this man died in a solitary hut near the banks of
Lake Rotorua. Being a lady of rank she was left
in her hut, the door and windows were made fast,
and the dwelling was abandoned, as her death
had made it tapu. But a day or two after, Te
Wharewera with some others paddling in a
canoe near the place at early morning saw a
figure on the shore beckoning to them. It was
the aunt come to life again, but weak and cold

and famished. When sufficiently restored by their timely help, she told her story. Leaving her body, her spirit had taken the flight toward the North Cape, and arrived at the entrance of Reigna. There, holding on by the stem of the creeping akeake plant, she descended the precipice, and found herself on the sandy beach of a river. Looking around, she espied in the distance an enormous bird, taller than a man, coming toward her with rapid strides. This terrible object so frightened her that her first thought was to try to return up the steep cliff; but seeing an old man padding a small canoe toward her she ran to meet him, and so escaped the bird. When she had been safely ferried across she asked the old Charon, mentioning the name of her family, where the spirits of her kindred dwelt. Following the path the old man pointed out, she was surprised to find it just such a path as she had been used to on earth; the aspect of the country, the trees, shrubs, and plants were all familiar to her. She reached the village and among the crowd assembled there she found her father and many near relations; they saluted her, and welcomed her with the wailing chant which Maoris always address to people met after long absence. But when her father had asked about his living relatives, and especially about her own child, he told her she must go back to earth, for no one was left to take care of his grandchild. By his orders she refused to touch the food that the dead people offered her, and in spite of their efforts to detain her, her father got her safely into the canoe, crossed with her, and parting gave her from under his cloak two enormous sweet potatoes to plant at home for his grandchild's especial eating. But as she began to climb the precipice again, two pursuing infant spirits pulled her back, and she only escaped by flinging the roots at them, which they stopped to eat, while she scaled the rock by help of the akeake stem, till she reached the earth and flew back to where she had left her body. On returning to life she found herself in darkness, and what had passed seemed as a dream, till she perceived that she was deserted and the door fast, and concluded that she had really died and come to life again. When morning dawned, a faint light entered by the crevices of the shut-up house, and she saw on the floor near her a calabash partly full of red ocher mixed with water; this she eagerly drained to the dregs, and then feeling a little stronger, succeeded in opening the door and crawling down to the beach, where her friends soon after found her. Those who listened to her tale firmly believed the reality of her adventures, but it was much regretted that she had not brought back at least one of the huge sweet potatoes as evidence of her visit to the land of spirits.[3]

I have been unable to find Edward Shortland's *Traditions and Superstitions of the New Zealanders*, from which Tylor summarizes. However, even allowing for cultural variation in expression and symbolization and for the garbling which probably took place as the story was passed from person to person, one recognizes several of the common elements of near-death experiences which have been discussed. The woman who "died" left her body, crossed a river, was met by departed relatives, and was told that she had to go back to care for her son.

The English writer Thomas De Quincey (1785–1859) was familiar with near-death experiences.

In *Confessions of an English Opium Eater* he describes his own problems with opium addiction, a habit which was quite widespread in his day, when opium was freely available and easily and legally purchased. He describes how sometimes scenes from his past would come back to him, and this reminds him of a story related to him by a female relative, widely believed by scholars to have been his mother.

In the first (1821) edition of his book, he writes:

> I was once told by a near relative of mine, that having in her childhood fallen into a river, and being on the very verge of death but for the critical assistance which reached her, she saw in a moment her whole life, in its minutest incidents, arrayed before her simultaneously as in a mirror; and she had a faculty developed as suddenly for comprehending the whole and every part.[4]

In a sequel, *Suspiria De Profundis*, De Quincey elaborates further on this incident and remarks on the skeptical response his retelling of it apparently elicited in some readers.

> The lady is still living, though now of unusually great age; and I may mention that among her faults never was numbered any levity of principle, or carelessness of the most scrupulous veracity; but, on the contrary, such faults as arise from austerity, too harsh, perhaps, and gloomy, indulgent neither to others nor herself. And, at the time of relating this incident, when already very old, she had become religious to asceticism. According to my present belief, she

had completed her ninth year, when, playing by
the side of a solitary brook, she fell into one of
its deepest pools. Eventually, but after what
lapse of time nobody ever knew, she was saved
from death by a farmer, who, riding in some
distant lane, had seen her rise to the surface;
but not until she had descended within the abyss
of death, and looked into its secrets, as far,
perhaps, as ever human eye *can* have looked that
had permission to return. At a certain stage of
this descent, a blow seemed to strike her;
phosphoric radiance sprang forth from her eye-
balls; and immediately a mighty theater ex-
panded within her brain. In a moment, in the
twinkling of an eye, every act, every design of
her past life, lived again, arraying themselves
not as a succession, but as parts of a coexistence.
Such a light fell upon the whole path of her life
backward into the shades of infancy as the light,
perhaps, which wrapt the destined apostle [Paul]
on his road to Damascus. Yet that light blinded
for a season; but hers poured celestial vision upon
the brain, so that her consciousness became
omnipresent at one moment to every feature in
the infinite review.

This anecdote was treated skeptically at the
time by some critics. But, besides that it has since
been confirmed by other experience essentially
the same, reported by other parties in the same
circumstances, who had never heard of each
other, the true point for astonishment is not the
*simultaneity* of arrangement under which the
past events of life, though in fact successive, had
formed their dread line of revelation. This was
but a secondary phenomenon; the deeper lay in
the resurrection itself, and the possibility of
resurrection, for what had so long slept in the
dust. A pall, deep as oblivion, had been thrown
by life over every trace of these experiences; and

yet suddenly, at a silent command, at the signal of a blazing rocket sent up from the brain, the pall draws up, and the whole depths of the theater are exposed.[5]

With respect to more recent times, it is noteworthy that members of the Church of Jesus Christ of Latter-Day Saints (the Mormons) have been aware of accounts of near-death experiences for many years and circulate these stories among themselves. Also interesting is the fact that the renowned psychiatrist Carl Gustav Jung had a near-death experience; he describes it in the section entitled "Visions" in the book *Memories, Dreams, and Reflections*.

Oscar Lewis, a contemporary anthropologist, wrote a fascinating work, *The Children of Sánchez*, based on his studies of life in a Mexican family. One of the members of the family related a near-death experience to him.

There are similar descriptions in literature. To give only two, Ernest Hemingway, in *A Farewell to Arms*, has the narrator describe how he had the sensation of being out of his body during a close call with death. (This is interesting in that some say that this novel is largely autobiographical.) And Count Leo Tolstoy, in *The Death of Ivan Ilyich*, describes the death scene of Ivan Ilyich in terms of being in a dark, cavelike space, of having a flashback of his past life, and at last, of entering into a brilliant light.

Again, the above are only a few of the many

accounts available. Far from being a new phenomenon, near-death experiences have been with us for a long, long time.

[1] Bede, *A History of the English Church and People*, trans. Leo Sherley-Price (Harmondsworth, England: Penguin Books, 1968), pp. 289–293.

[2] Kenneth Hurlstone Jackson, *A Celtic Miscellany* (London, England: Routledge & Kegan Paul, Ltd., 1971), pp. 285–287.

[3] Edward Burnett Tylor, *Primitive Culture*, Vol. II (New York: Henry Holt and Co., 1874), pp. 50–52.

[4] Thomas De Quincey, *Confessions of an English Opium Eater with Its Sequels Suspiria De Profundis and The English Mail-Coach*, ed. Malcolm Elwin (London: Macdonald & Co., 1956), pp. 420–421.

[5] Ibid., pp. 511–512.

# 6
# MORE QUESTIONS

Since the publication of *Life After Life*, I have received many questions from readers of the book, from medical and academic colleagues, and from other interested individuals. I feel that many of these questions are of general interest, and so I shall answer them through the forum of this second book.

*Won't the broad public discussion of the details of this phenomenon interfere with the accuracy of future research in this area?*

This is a difficult issue, of course. It does raise the specter not only of subsequent experiences being shaped by reading accounts of earlier ones, but also the possibility that unscrupulous persons may falsely allege that they have been through such experiences in order to attract attention and publicity, or to achieve some other dubious advantage. However, even though my study and those of Dr. Kubler-Ross and other investigators in this field may complicate the problem of separating the wheat from the chaff, I still think that if the phenomenon is ever to be studied scientifically it must first be brought to the foreground.

The alternative is to keep it a professional secret and this, too, is full of objections and perplexities. For years the question very frequently asked me has been, "If such things are so commonly experienced, why haven't they been more widely publicized?" Now, it's beginning to appear that we might go through a time in which the question will be, "Since such things are so widely publicized, is it any wonder that they're so commonly experienced?"

*Why don't you use the names of the people you have interviewed? Wouldn't this make your work more credible?*

It will continue to be my policy not to use names. There are several reasons for this. People have come to me under the assumption that I would not be using their names. I want to continue this practice so that I can continue collecting accounts which people might not give me if they felt that they would be identified. It might well make more tantalizing reading if I were to print a picture of a person and give out his name and address, as one might do in a newspaper article. However, this would not make my study more credible from a scientific point of view.

What will make this more real, ultimately, is for others to find the same things I have in different cases. In my book I draw no conclusions: I only make a prediction that others who pursue this matter sympathetically and diligently will be able to find examples of near-death experiences which demonstrate all of the various elements and stages of the experiences about which I have written.

*Isn't this whole concept of life after death just so much wishful thinking?*

Some might argue that since all, or at least, most of us, would wish to live after death, any evidence which is presented to that effect should be regarded suspiciously. Such arguments abound in many quarters, but I might point out that this can work the other way, too. The fact that there is something that most of us desire does not imply that it does not occur.

William James put it very well when he said, in effect, that with respect to religious matters which are not susceptible to empirical proof or disproof, it did not appear any more rational to disbelieve them out of fear of being wrong than it was to believe out of hope of being right.

*Isn't interest in near-death experiences just a "fad"?*

I doubt it. Concern with the nature and meaning of death has endured throughout the history of Western thought. Almost all of the great philosophers have dealt with this issue, and it can be seen almost as the central theme of the writings and systems of many of them.

Secondly, the rapid progress in resuscitation

technology almost guarantees that we will be dealing with this phenomenon increasingly in the future.

Finally, many doctors must have heard from terminally ill patients the anguished plea, "Can't anyone tell me what it is like to die?" Regardless of whether one conceives of near-death experiences as intimations of immortality or merely as the result of terminal physiological events, I think that it is a gain that we are beginning to be able to shed a little more light on that question.

*Were the people with whom you have talked interested in the occult either prior to or after their experience?*

I have talked with more than three hundred people now who have had near-death experiences. In a group that size it is not surprising that one would find a few who did have some sort of interest in such matters as reincarnation, communication with spirits through mediums, astrology, and other occult phenomena. However, it is quite interesting to me that out of my group of subjects, only six or seven expressed any sort of interest in this area, either before or after their experience. Almost none of these people have reported having more than one uncanny or unusual experience in the course of their lives.

By and large, the people with whom I have talked are not people who frequently have unusual experiences, or who have any more than the average interest in occult matters.

*Have you ever interviewed any atheists who had these experiences?*

Everyone with whom I have talked came from within the Judeo-Christian tradition.

In that context, the word "atheist" is, at least in part, a "judgmental" term that entails a certain interpretation of personality, feelings, and belief. "Atheism" may be, in some cases, just verbal behavior masking personal feelings that may be very different, perhaps even deeply religious.

I feel that it would be almost impossible to determine the degree of prior religious belief in these cases, since everyone in our society is at least exposed to religious concepts. In view of this, the question would always arise for any person to what degree—even unconsciously—he already holds to religious concepts.

The persons I interviewed who stated that they had no particular religious beliefs prior to their near-death experiences, did state that after having this experience they now accept as true the religious doctrines of a hereafter.

*What was the age range of the persons whom you interviewed?*

I have talked with several adults who were telling me of experiences which took place when they were children. The youngest age in these reports was three years. However, I have talked to only one child who told me of his experience and this was quite by coincidence. He just happened to tell it to me in a pediatrics clinic when I was helping to treat him.

The oldest person with whom I have talked was approximately seventy-five at the time of his experience. He told it to me only about two months later. It seems to me that the age of the person has little to do with the content of the experience. Of course, the thoughts which go through a child's mind at this time of crisis are different from those which occur to an adult, and he may express them differently.

*Isn't the effect of all this to glorify death?*

No, absolutely not. I think that we all recognize the bad aspects of death. Death is bad in its aspects of separation from loved ones and in the suffering from illness or injury that can take place before it. It is also bad in that people may die prematurely before having a chance to complete things which they want to accomplish in life.

*I "died" and was resuscitated. Yet, I remember nothing at all about it. What's wrong with me?*

Several people have expressed this kind of worry to me, and in response I want to take the opportunity to make several remarks. As I emphasized in *Life After Life*, not everyone who survives a clinical "death" remembers anything whatsoever about it. I have talked with many people who remember nothing about it.

I can't detect *any* difference between those who do and those who don't have such experiences during their "death" in their religious background or personality, in the circumstances or cause of "death," or in any other factor.

One wonders whether a certain percentage of the people who remember nothing might not be suppressing this material, that is, whether there might not have been an experience at the time which the subconscious mind, for one reason or another, forced the conscious mind to "forget."

I want very much for others to avoid taking my list of common elements as being a fixed, exhaustive model of what a near-death experience *must* be like. There is an enormously wide spectrum of experiences, with some people having only one or two of the elements, and others most of them. I anticipate that the list I have developed will be added to, modified, and reformulated. Such a list is only intended as a rough-and-ready theoretical model, and one ought to avoid any temptation of making it into a fixed ideal.

*You say that not everyone who goes through an apparent clinical death has any experience. What percentage do?*

The kind of study which I have done does not give me a basis on which to make such a judgment. In the first place, my sample of cases is obviously weighted toward those who did have an experience. Due to the nature of what I am doing, those who have experiences would be more likely to tell me about them than would those who went through a clinical death and remember nothing.

A similar question has been often posed about the individual elements of near-death experiences. People ask, for instance, what percentage of the people report going through the tunnel or seeing the being of light, etc. I have not attempted to calculate what percentage of people report each element. Firstly, one cannot be sure that because a person didn't include a given element in recounting his experience, the element wasn't present. He may have forgotten it, or had some reason for omitting it. Secondly, I haven't bothered to count because such an exercise would yield only pseudoscientific number magic.

It would have been a simple matter to have illustrated both my books with graphs and charts showing such figures and percentages. However, since my sample of cases is not random and was not collected under controlled circumstances, such graphs and charts would only represent self-deception and have no scientific validity.

The only way questions such as these could be answered satisfactorily from a scientific point of view would be to do prospective studies of the kind which I will try to describe more fully in the Appendix. For example, the next 250 cases of successful cardiopulmonary resuscitation attempts in a given hospital might be investigated under given controlled conditions to test given experimental hypotheses.

In spite of the lack of statistical evidence, I feel that near-death experiences of the type I have described are common among persons who have been resuscitated. I predict that any investigator who enters into this type of study sympathetically and diligently will find that there is ample case material.

*Have you ever interviewed a person about a near-death experience by placing him under hypnosis?*

I once thought that, given willing subjects, this could conceivably be a fruitful avenue to follow. In fact, I was in the preliminary stages of planning an investigation of this sort with the cooperation of a skilled and experienced medical hypnotist. However, it occurred to us that, theoretically, attempting to take a person back in time to the moment of his clinical death could be dangerous. The subconscious mind takes hypnotic suggestions very literally. In addition, hypnotic suggestions can have surprising and odd effects on the body and its function. For example, it is said that a blister may be raised on the skin of a hypnotized person merely by suggesting that a very hot object has been touched to his skin.

Considering this, we thought that in obeying the suggestion to go back mentally to the moment of a clinical "death," a person could literally go through the physiological events of death again. So we never tried our experiment. Just recently, I have learned of an experiment of this kind in which the patient actually did go into cardiac failure and had to be brought out of it! Needless to say, such experiments are to be frowned upon.

*Should one tell terminally ill patients about these experiences?*

Several physicians have asked me this. I have never resolved it satisfactorily in my own mind, since there are so many variables. On the negative side, one could argue that this knowledge might disturb people who have a fixed theology which holds that very different kinds of events unfold after death—or that no events at all transpire. In this case, one can well argue that one should not tell them because it may disturb them, especially if they have already made their peace with death in their own fashion.

On the other hand, I have heard it argued that there are some people who should be told. If these reports are not true and there is no life after death, no harm was done. But if the reports are true, people might be better prepared for what lies ahead for them. *The Tibetan Book of the Dead* was apparently written for this purpose. One idea behind it was that it could be read to those who were dying (and, for a while after they died) so that they would be less confused about the states through which they were going.

I think the ultimate answer to this question depends on the persons involved. Physicians would have to depend upon their clinical judgment, their knowledge of what kind of person their patient is, and the particular doctor-patient relationship that exists.

At any rate, this question may soon be academic, since it appears that the fact that such experiences occur is becoming increasingly known. In this regard, I might mention a proposal made by a pediatrician who has dealt with many terminally ill patients. She suggests that people who have had near-death experiences share them with terminally ill persons who express an interest in hearing about them.

*How should one respond when an acquaintance (or a patient) reports such an experience without being asked?*

This question has presented itself to me in a very personal way. Curiously enough, I have never interviewed a patient whom I helped to resuscitate. However, during the course of my medical education, I did have two patients who spontaneously described near-death experiences to me. In both cases, the experiences had taken place some months earlier and in neither case had I asked the patient anything connected with this topic. They simply recounted their experiences in the course of the usual kind of conversation that goes on between doctor and patient.

I found both these events striking in that they provided further confirmation of my belief that one reason that physicians have not heretofore noticed this phenomenon very much is that they simply don't hear it when patients tell them about such occurrences.

One of the patients was an elderly man with a skin problem; the other was a retarded twelve-year-old boy who had a congenital endocrine disease. Neither knew that I had been doing a study of near-death experiences. I was so taken aback at the unexpectedness of these disclosures that what I ended up doing, in effect, was nothing.

In each instance, I made some innocuous remark like "That's interesting," and didn't press the matter further. I suppose I felt at the time that these patients were there for help with a specific medical problem and that the clinic was not the appropriate place to pursue this kind of discussion. I gave no indication to either patient that I had ever heard of such an experience before.

As I look back, I have a sense of guilt that I did not share my knowledge of these experiences with these two people. Perhaps hearing that these experiences had also happened to others would have been the most important kind of support that I could have given them.

My present feeling is that, again depending on the particular relationship involved, one might respond by saying something along the following lines: "Such experiences occur, and many have reported them. Though from a scientific and medical standpoint, one cannot make a specific statement about what they represent, the experience must have meant a great deal to you. Ultimately it will be for you to understand it and integrate it into your own life. You may find help in gaining understanding by reading great religious writings and by discussions with other people who have had these experiences or who have investigated or thought about them."

*Should the fact that one knows about such experiences affect one's care of a dying patient?*

This is a very complex issue. One thing that occurs to me is that one should be very careful about what is said at resuscitation attempts, even when it seems obvious that the patient is lost. Many physicians have been surprised to hear their remarks quoted to them by the patient after a successful resuscitation attempt. I know of one physician who in his practice deals with many terminally ill patients. He knew of many experiences of the kind I have written about even before he read of my research. He has developed the practice of staying with his patients for a while after they have died and taking care of them by talking to them. Interestingly, he does this even though he personally believes near-death experiences represent nothing more than physiological processes that continue in the brain for a while even after the heart has stopped beating.

*What implications do studies of near-death phenomena have for the ethical issues surrounding maintaining life artificially, even after brain function has been unalterably impaired?*

The implications of these studies may be very important for cases in which life is sustained artificially. However, the state of the research in this area is so elementary right now that no conclusions whatsoever can be drawn. Even if the reality of near-death phenomena were to come to be taken as established scientific fact, and not a matter lying in the realm of anecdote and speculation, these ethical dilemmas would still exist.

With respect to the specific question concerning so-called "mercy killing," however, my opinion is more dogmatic. I am opposed to it on ethical grounds and would not recommend it under any conditions.

*I am a member of an emergency medical team and am frequently involved in trying to revive patients with essentially no vital signs. It is troubling to learn from these patients, as one occasionally does, that they resented the efforts to bring them back because they were having one of these experiences. How is one to deal emotionally with this?*

I've heard stories, too, both from patients and from doctors, about happenings like this. However, in my experience, this has been a temporary response. They might resent the resuscitation measures at the time, but from the perspective of a few hours, days, or weeks, their attitude changes. They, by and large, become very grateful that they have been given "a second chance."

*Some of your subjects have said that they came to believe that the ability to love others and the accumulation of knowledge were the two most important goals to seek in life. Could you elaborate more fully on this? What kind of love? What kind of knowledge?*

Both "love" and "knowledge" are English words which are highly ambiguous. The Greek words *philos, eros,* and *agapē,* despite the fact that they express very different concepts, could all three be translated into English as "love"! I gather from the tone of the persons who report these experiences that the kind of love they have in mind is probably closest to the concept of *agapē*. It can be characterized, generally, as an overflowing, spontaneous, unmotivated kind of love which is given to others regardless of their faults.

Similarly, the Greek words *epistēmē* and *technē*, again with very different meanings, would both be translated as "knowledge." *Technē*, as is implied in the use of its English cognates "technology" and "technique," has partly to do with what one might call the application of knowledge. *Epistēmē* deals more with factual and theoretical kinds of knowledge. My impression from listening to stories of near-death experiences is that the kind of knowledge people mean has more to do with theoretical and factual kinds of things. No one seems to have come back, for instance, with the impassioned desire to learn how to ride a bicycle, despite the fact that one can talk in English of "knowing" how to ride a bicycle.

Recently I have been asking people who have had near-death experiences to explain as well as they could what kind of love or knowledge they felt was important. One subject was a man in his forties who had been involved in a severe automobile accident. He was taken to a hospital where his condition was declared hopeless, but he was resuscitated. In an interview which took place about a month later, he said the following:

[About love] Now, he asked me about love. How far had I learned to love? What he was asking was obvious to me then, but it is so hard to explain now. He wanted me to understand that it was the kind of love that has nothing to do with downgrading people. Could I love people, even when I knew them really well, even their faults, was what he was asking.

[About knowledge] The knowledge that I had gained: that was mentioned, too. . . . What kind of knowledge? Well, it's hard to say, you know. But it was knowledge of basic things, causes of things, the basic universal principles . . . of things that hold the universe together. . . . I was told that that would be important over there, too. . . .

The following excerpts are from an interview with a housewife in her late thirties who had developed complications after surgery and suffered a heart arrest.

[About love] He showed me all that I had done, and then he asked me if I was satisfied with my life. . . . He was interested in love. Love was it. And he meant the kind of love that makes me want to know if my neighbor is fed and clothed and makes me want to help him, if he is not.

[About knowledge] The kind of knowledge meant was deeper knowledge, sort of as it related to the soul . . . wisdom, I would say.

It is quite clear that love was the goal that was most emphasized in the reviews of their lives which these two people witnessed. When knowledge was mentioned by the being of light, it was often done in a casual and almost offhand way. He implied that learning was not something that stopped at people's death but would continue even when they came over there permanently.

Bear in mind that this discussion is complicated by the fact that people say that in order to express the full impact of the experience, they would need language far beyond their capabilities. The words they are able to use are inadequate. Indeed, the ultimate realities are ineffable.

There is another Greek word, *sophia*, which also has to do with knowledge. *Sophia* would be translated into English as "wisdom," and it is significant that precisely this term comes up in one of the accounts quoted above. *Sophia* and "wisdom" alike have—if one may put it this way—an ethical dimension as well as a factual one. The wise man, presumably, would not only possess knowledge but would be able to apply it in a morally correct way. So the account quoted implies a moral aspect to the accumulation of knowledge.

*Can't people have similar or the same experiences as you have described without "dying" or even coming near death?*

Yes, apparently so. Many people have told me of out-of-body experiences which took place spontaneously. The persons involved were not "dead" or even ill or in jeopardy. Further, in most cases these experiences were not being sought out in any way. They came as complete surprises.

Near-death experiences are also similar in many respects to mystical and religious visions described by great seers in the past. Many more examples of similarities could, no doubt, be cited. However, I have not sought out such accounts or followed up the ones that were reported to me. This is not because I am not interested in them. It is just that I have found more than enough material to keep me busy concentrating on those in which a near-death encounter does take place.

If I were asked how I account for these similarities and allowed to be wildly speculative, I could think of any number of possible explanations. For example, let us take as a hypothesis that there is a direct continuation of life after physical death. If this is so, there must be some mechanism —bodily or spiritual or maybe both—that releases the psyche, the soul (or whatever one wants to call it), from the body upon physical death. Now, we don't assume that our bodily mechanisms work perfectly every time. The organs of our body sometimes malfunction and our reason, perception, or thinking may sometimes lead us astray. Analogously, we have no reason to assume that this hypothetical mechanism for releasing the soul from the body always would work perfectly. Might it not be that different kinds of situations—stresses, etc.—could sometimes work to set off this mechanism prematurely? If all this were true, then it could explain the similarity between near-death experiences and other kinds, such as out-of-body experiences. It could also explain the fact that the phenomena reported by those who find themselves in life-threatening situations without even being injured can be identical with the experiences of those who are revived after an apparent clinical "death."

*You have just said that mystical visions are similar in many respects to near-death experiences. What are the points of similarity?*

Many people these days seem to regard "mysticism" as synonymous with "Oriental mysticism." However, there is a long history of mystical visions in the Western tradition. St. Augustine, St. Francis of Assisi, Teresa of Avila, Meister Eckhardt, and John of Arc all could be called mystics.

In his famous study *The Varieties of Religious Experience*, William James gives the following list of the characteristics of mystical visions.

> 1. *Ineffability*—The handiest of the marks by which I classify a state of mind as mystical is negative. The subject of it immediately says that it defies expression, that no adequate report of its contents can be given in words. . . .
> 2. *Noetic quality*—Mystical states seem to those who experience them to be also states of knowledge. They are states of insight into depths of truth unplumbed by the discursive intellect. . . .
> These two characters will entitle any state to be called mystical, in the sense in which I use the word. Two other qualities are less sharply marked, but are usually found. These are:—
> 3. *Transiency*—Mystical states cannot be sustained for long. Except in rare instances, half an hour, or at most an hour or two, seems to be the limit beyond which they fade into the light of common day. . . .

4. *Passivity*—Although the oncoming of mystical states may be facilitated by preliminary voluntary operations, as by fixing the attention, or going through certain bodily performances, or in other ways which manuals of mysticism prescribe; yet when the characteristic sort of consciousness once has set in, the mystic feels as if his own will were in abeyance, and indeed sometimes as if he were grasped and held by a superior power. This latter peculiarity connects mystical states with certain definite phenomena of secondary or alternative personality, such as prophetic speech, automatic writing, or the mediumistic trance. When these latter conditions are well pronounced, however, there may be no recollection whatever of the phenomenon, and it may have no significance for the subject's usual inner life, to which, as it were, it makes a mere interruption. Mystical states, strictly so called, are never merely interruptive. Some memory of their content always remains, and a profound sense of their importance. They modify the inner life of the subject between the times of their recurrence. Sharp divisions in this region are, however, difficult to make, and we find all sorts of gradations and mixtures.[1]

Others have pointed out additional characteristics. Two examples are the occurrence of an altered sense of time and space and an integrating effect—in many cases—of the vision on the personality and subsequent life of the individual.

All of the criteria above obviously apply in one way or another to the case of near-death experiences. However, there are other very common features of near-death experiences which have not figured prominently as aspects of the experiences of the great mystics of history. The panoramic review of one's life is an example.

*Do people say that their sense of time is changed during these experiences?*

It is very commonly reported that during near-death experiences, time is altered. This comes much to the fore in remarks like that of one woman who during an apparent clinical "death" seemed to find herself in paradisiacal surroundings. When I asked how long this seemed to take she said, "You could say a minute or you could say ten thousand years. It doesn't make any difference."

Again, a man who was trapped in an explosion and fire seemed to float above his body and to see others as they ran to rescue him. He says that at this point his physical surroundings seemed to disappear entirely and a review of his entire life came before him, while he "discussed" it in the presence of "Christ." When asked how long the review seemed to take, he remarked that if he were forced to put it in temporal terms he would have to say that it took an hour at the very least. Yet, when he was told he must return and the review disappeared, he again saw his physical surroundings. The persons he saw coming to rescue him seemed frozen in stop motion, in the same positions they had been just as the review started. When he seemed to be returning to his body, the action speeded up again.

These examples and many more illustrate how, during near-death experiences, to use the words of yet another person, "Time there isn't like time here." One might point to this as yet another feature in which near-death experiences resemble mystical visions.

*Do people who are out of their bodies during near-death experiences feel pain?*

Many people have told me that while they felt they were out of their bodies they sensed no pain whatsoever, even though they may have been in great pain just prior to this. Some have reported with amazement that even though they could see their physicians or other medical personnel pounding on their chests, sticking IV needles into their arms, etc., while in the out-of-body state, they felt no pain at all from these activities. On the other hand, people have reported that as soon as they re-entered their bodies, they were immediately seized again by pain.

*You have mentioned cases of near-death experiences of extreme duration. How is it possible that these people were revived without serious brain damage?*

Several facts could be brought up here. First of all, during resuscitation procedures, the brain *is* being perfused with blood and with the oxygen and nourishment it carries. This is the point of cardiac massage: to keep the blood flowing even though the heart is not beating by itself.

Secondly, conditions such as variations in temperature can affect the rate at which the brain may be damaged. The brain of a person who had a temperature of 105° just prior to death would deteriorate more rapidly than that of a person whose body temperature had been lowered. Indeed, during operations such as open heart surgery the heart has been stopped for long periods without the person's brain being perfused, without attendant brain damage. This was made possible by the use of hypothermic techniques; the brain temperature was artificially lowered.

So, although many have heard that after five minutes without oxygen resuscitation without brain damage is impossible, this is only a simplified rule. All sorts of other factors must be taken into account in considering the complex circumstances of a resuscitation attempt. Indeed, severe brain damage is not usual among patients who are revived after a cardiac arrest.

*You have said that near-death experiences have become much more common in recent decades due to developments in resuscitation techniques. Was there any kind of resuscitation before the advent of modern medicine?*

Resuscitation itself, in one form or another, is a very ancient technique. Phoenician medical tablets thousands of years old have described techniques of resuscitation by mouth-to-mouth respiration. Also, we find in *The Bible*, in II Kings 4:18–37, the following rather remarkable narrative.

> And when the child was grown, it fell on a day, that he went out to his father to the reapers, and he said unto his father, My head, my head. And he said to a lad, carry him to his mother.

And when he had taken him, and brought him to his mother, he sat on her knees till noon, and then died. And she went up, and laid him on the bed of the man of God, and shut the door upon him, and went out. . . . Then she saddled an ass, and said to her servant, Drive, and go forward . . . So she went and came unto the man of God . . . And he arose, and followed her. . . . And when Elisha was come into the house, behold the child was dead, and laid upon his bed. He went in therefore, and shut the door upon them twain, and prayed unto the Lord. And he went up, and lay upon the child, and put his mouth upon his mouth, and his eyes upon his eyes, and his hands upon his hands; and he stretched himself upon the child; and the flesh of the child waxed warm. Then he returned, and walked in the house to and fro; and went up, and stretched himself upon him: and the child sneezed seven times, and the child opened his eyes. . . . And when she [the mother] was come in unto him, he said, Take up thy son. Then she went in, and fell at his feet, and bowed herself to the ground, and took up her son, and went out.

A similar but somewhat less detailed story is found in I Kings 17. An interesting detail in the passage from II Kings just quoted is that the boy sneezed upon being revived. It is a folk belief of many peoples that a sneeze is a sign that the soul has re-entered the body after having briefly left it. This otherwise puzzling little detail is probably a reflection of this belief.

Among techniques of resuscitation known and used in very early times was applying heat to the abdomen of the victim. Another was flagellation; pain was inflicted on the unconscious person by flogging him with nettles in hopes of reviving him. No doubt other methods were used as well, but a significant advance, which may seem more "scientific" to contemporary minds, was achieved by the Renaissance physician Paracelsus, a German who lived from 1493 until 1541. He introduced the procedure of resuscitating the apparently dead or near-dead by forcing air into their lungs with the common bellows—which was, then as now, used by the fireplace. Vesalius (1514–1564), another outstanding physician of that period, also used the bellows for resuscitation and did experiments with artificial respiration. The bellows method was subsequently used in Europe for several centuries. Many other techniques, including rolling a nearly drowned person over a barrel, and laying a person over the back of a horse and trotting the horse, have been used over the centuries in different societies. The method of restarting the heart by injections of adrenalin (epinephrine) was developed as long ago as 1905 by Winter.

Techniques of resuscitation have a long history, not only in Western and Judeo-Christian societies but also in what we call "primitive" cultures. For example, some Indians of North America used a method in which smoke contained in a syringe-like instrument was forced into the victim's rectum. Despite the fact that this technique sounds implausible, it is alleged that it was used successfully in the American colonies for some time and was introduced into Great Britain in the latter part of the eighteenth century.

Since close calls with death are common in

every society from the most primitive to the most highly developed, I have wondered whether the occurrence of near-death experiences might not be part of the explanation for a certain very ancient and widespread concept of disease. All over the world, and far back into history, many have believed that in certain instances sickness was caused by the soul's leaving the body. Where such beliefs are accepted, treatment is directed toward persuading or forcing the patient to get back into his body. One can point to other such folk beliefs—for example, that of the inhabitants of central Celebes, an island in eastern Indonesia, that the soul may leave the body when a person is suddenly and unexpectedly frightened—and wonder whether these beliefs did not come about partly because of near-death experiences much like the ones with which I have been dealing.

*What have you found the attitude of physicians to be toward these experiences?*

Again, as in the case of ministers, physicians are an enormously varied group of human beings, made up of individuals with different backgrounds, interests, and personalities. So, predictably, the response from them has been quite diverse. Nonetheless, it falls fairly neatly into about four categories, which makes the task of discussion somewhat easier.

The first group consists of physicians who have had this experience themselves. Their attitude toward these experiences does not seem to be any different from that of anyone else who has had a near-death experience. A point that two physicians have made in relating their own accounts is that, despite the overwhelming reality of what they were experiencing, there was little in their scientific background that had prepared them for understanding it, or that gave them a language in which to express it. When I asked one doctor about his attitude to his own out-of-body experience, he answered, "As a scientist, I would've thought it couldn't happen. But it really did!"

A second group consists of the doctors who have contacted me to tell me of their own patients who had reported these experiences. Several physicians have remarked that they, too, had been collecting these accounts, had been quite baffled by them, and were glad to find out that others had been doing research into this area.

Yet another group has expressed a religious attitude toward these phenomena. They feel that the occurrence of near-death experiences confirms their own religious faith that there is a continuation of life after physical death.

A fourth group consists of physicians who feel that near-death experiences are reducible to medical phenomena with which we are already familiar. They feel, in short, that they can explain near-death experiences on the basis of what we already know scientifically about physiology and/or psychology.

*What are some examples of known medical phenomena which have been proposed as explanations of these experiences?*

There is an almost endless list of conditions known to medicine which can produce experiences that, in one respect or another, resemble the phenomena reported in some near-death encounters. In *Life After Life*, I discussed certain pharmacological, physiological, neurological, and psychological explanations of near-death experiences. It would be pointless to explore each of the possible explanations separately, but I will remark that the two fields of medicine which seem to be among the most fertile grounds from which phenomena similar to near-death experiences are derived are anesthesiology and neurology. I am aware, of course, that sensations like that of being drawn down a dark tunnel are often reported by persons being placed under anesthetics—especially ether. Yet, I do not believe that anesthetic effects constitute a valid, complete explanation of near-death experiences, since very few of my subjects were under any sort of anesthetic at the time the experience took place.

Likewise, many neurologists have pointed out to me over the past several years that near-death experiences bear a certain resemblance to seizure disorders, particularly to temporal lobe seizures. Some obvious points of resemblance are: (1) People who have temporal lobe seizures may report that a "noise" heralds the onset of the episode. (2) The temporal lobe has a role in memory, and persons who have approached death may talk of panoramic memory.

One could continue almost indefinitely drawing further parallels. For example, one might postulate that the impression of intense light reported by these persons is the result simply of events caused by interference with oxygen supply to the occipital lobes (the area of the brain which is the "seat" of vision). I would like to add to the list (besides those, such as autoscopy, mentioned in *Life After Life*) the experiences reported to the famous neurosurgeon Dr. Wilder Penfield by some of his patients. In a classic series of experiments, Dr. Penfield stimulated certain areas of the brains of his patients while they were undergoing brain surgery. When he did this, he found that very vivid memories—actually a sort of reliving of events—would flood into the patient's consciousness. Precise, complete details of events which had occurred years before could be recovered.

Yet, I personally remain unconvinced that these well-known neurological phenomena "explain" near-death experiences. Consider the explanation in terms of seizures, for example. Such attempted explanations are almost invariably based upon the premise that "cerebral anoxia" (loss of oxygen to the brain) is the specific cause of the seizure discharge. However, this neglects the point that all the phenomena alluded to—the noise, the panoramic memory, and the light—have been experienced in the course of near-death encounters in which this cut-off of blood flow to the brain never took place. Remember that I emphasized from the beginning that I have dealt with some near-death experiences in which no apparent clinical death took place, and that these contain many of the same features as those in which there

was such a "death." A simple review of the cases
I have presented should make this point obvious.

Some might want to go further and try to explain
near-death experiences in which the light, the
review, and other phenomena were experienced
without any compromise of brain oxygen supply
by saying that in these cases it was the "stress" of
the close encounter with death which set off the
alleged brain events. My only feeling about this
is that here the concept of "stress" has been so
stretched as to be almost without any explanatory
force. ("What *kind* of stress?", one might ask.)

It is quite easy to go on formulating explanations of this type endlessly. However, it is also all
too easy to accept some such explanation as
obvious without giving proper attention to elements of near-death experiences which do not fit
the suggested explanation. For example, physicians
have reported to me that they just can't understand how their patients could have described the
things they did about the resuscitation efforts
unless they really were hovering just below the
ceiling. Numerous persons have told me that while
they were out of their bodies during apparent
"death," they witnessed events at a distance—
even outside the hospital—which were later confirmed by the reports of independent observers.
I think we ought at least to leave our minds open
to the possibility that such uncanny corroborations
might some day be produced under controlled experimental circumstances.

Finally, I must observe that such explanations
do not impress people who have had these experi-

ences themselves. One young man who was revived after an apparent "death" reflects:

> It's funny. It's something that there is no way that it could possibly exist, and yet you know without a doubt that it does.
>
> Now I know that a lot of people will not believe this. . . . People will come out and say that scientifically this cannot exist. . . . But, you know what? It won't change a thing. Because just as sure as I'm sitting here now, if I died again today, virtually the same thing would happen, except that I could observe it better. And they can tell me it's not, and they can swear that it's not, and they can show me scientific evidence that it's not . . . and all I can do is say, "Well, I know where I've been."

*What is your own personal attitude toward this research? Has it affected your life in any way?*

I find that even after I have asserted that I am not trying to prove that there is life after death and have made all of my usual qualifying remarks, some people with whom I talk are still not satisfied. They want to know what I, Raymond Moody, *feel.* I believe this is a legitimate question, as long as it is understood that this is a psychological matter and not a matter of a logical conclusion that I am trying to force on anyone else. To those who are interested in this autobiographical detail, I address the following remarks: I have come to accept as a matter of religious faith that there is a life after death, and I believe that the phenomenon we have been examining is a manifestation of that life.

However, far from being obsessed with death, I want to live. The persons I have interviewed would agree. The focus of their attention, as a result of having been through this experience, is on living. For we are all in this life now. At the same time, I hope to be able to apply what I have learned in this study to my life. I want to go on developing, as far as I can, in the areas of loving others and acquiring knowledge and wisdom.

Also, I am particularly concerned that near-death experiences not be perverted by using them as an excuse to form a new cult. This phenomenon should not be identified with me or with anyone else who has studied it. The near-death experience is very prevalent, and different perspectives are needed to cope with all of its complexities.

Finally, I have recently come to realize that my long contact with this research has resulted in my having a rather unusual distinction: A large percentage of my friends have been "dead!" Through talking with so many of these people, I have begun to realize how near to death we all are in our daily lives. More than ever now I am very careful to let each person I love know how I feel.

1 William James, *The Varieties of Religious Experience* (New York: New American Library, 1958), pp. 292–294.

# EPILOGUE

In Book VII of *The Republic*, the philosopher Plato (428–348 B.C.) produced for us a very powerful and beautiful allegory, which has since come to be known as the myth of the Cave. It takes the form of a dialogue between Plato's old teacher, Socrates, and another man, Glaucon. I quote this remarkable parable here without further comment. Its relevance is obvious.

Picture men dwelling in a sort of subterranean cavern with a long entrance open to the light on its entire width. Conceive them as having their legs and necks fettered from childhood, so that they remain in the same spot, able to look forward only, and prevented by the fetters from turning their heads. Picture further the light from a fire burning higher up and at a distance behind them, and between the fire and the prisoners and above them a road along which a low wall has been built, as the exhibitors of puppet shows have partitions before the men themselves, above which they show the puppets.

All that I see, he said.

See also, then, men carrying past the wall im-

plements of all kinds that rise above the wall,
and human images and shapes of animals as well,
wrought in stone and wood and every material,
some of these bearers presumably speaking and
others silent.

A strange image you speak of, he said, and
strange prisoners.

Like to us, I said. For, to begin with, tell me
do you think that these men would have seen
anything of themselves or of one another except
the shadows cast from the fire on the wall of the
cave that fronted them?

How could they, he said, if they were compelled to hold their heads unmoved through life?

And again, would not the same be true of the
objects carried past them?

Surely.

If then they were able to talk to one another,
do you not think that they would suppose that in
naming the things that they saw they were naming the passing objects?

Necessarily.

And if their prison had an echo from the wall
opposite them, when one of the passers-by ut-
tered a sound, do you think that they would
suppose anything else than the passing shadow
to be the speaker?

By Zeus, I do not, said he.

Then in every way such prisoners would deem
reality to be nothing else than the shadows of
the artificial objects.

Quite inevitably, he said.

Consider, then, what would be the manner of
the release and healing from these bonds and this
folly if in the course of nature something of this
sort should happen to them. When one was freed
from his fetters and compelled to stand up
suddenly and turn his head around and walk and
to lift up his eyes to the light, and in doing all

this felt pain and, because of the dazzle and glitter of the light, was unable to discern the objects whose shadows he formerly saw, what do you suppose would be his answer if someone told him that what he had seen before was all a cheat and an illusion, but that now, being nearer to reality and turned toward more real things, he saw more truly? And if also one should point out to him each of the passing objects and constrain him by questions to say what it is, do you not think that he would be at a loss and that he would regard what he formerly saw as more real than the things now pointed out to him?

Far more real, he said.

And if he were compelled to look at the light itself, would not that pain his eyes, and would he not turn away and flee to those things which he is able to discern and regard them as in very deed more clear and exact than the objects pointed out?

It is so, he said.

And if, said I, someone should drag him thence by force up the ascent which is rough and steep, and not let him go before he had drawn him out into the light of the sun, do you not think that he would find it painful to be so haled along, and would chafe at it, and when he came out into the light, that his eyes would be filled with its beams so that he would not be able to see even one of the things that we call real?

Why, no, not immediately, he said.

Then there would be need of habituation, I take it, to enable him to see the things higher up. And at first he would most easily discern the shadows and, after that, the likenesses or reflections in water of men and other things, and later, the things themselves, and from these he would go on to contemplate the appearances in the heavens and heaven itself, more easily by night, looking at the light of the stars and the moon, than by day the sun and the sun's light.

Of course.

And so, finally, I suppose, he would be able to look upon the sun itself and see its true nature, not by reflections in water or phantasms of it in an alien setting, but in and by itself in its own place.

Necessarily, he said.

And at this point he would infer and conclude that this it is that provides the seasons and the courses of the year and presides over all things in the visible region, and is in some sort the cause of all these things that they had seen.

Obviously, he said, that would be the next step.

Well then, if he recalled to mind his first habitation and what passed for wisdom there, and his fellow bondsmen, do you not think that he would count himself happy in the change and pity them?

He would indeed.

And if there had been honors and commendations among them which they bestowed on one another and prizes for the man who is quickest to make out the shadows as they pass and best able to remember their customary precedences, sequences, and coexistences, and so most successful in guessing at what was to come, do you think he would be very keen about such rewards, and that he would envy and emulate those who were honored by these prisoners and lorded it among them, or that he would feel with Homer and greatly prefer while living on earth to be serf of another, a landless man, and endure anything rather than opine with them and live that life?

Yes, he said, I think that he would choose to endure anything rather than such a life.

And consider this also, said I. If such a one should go down again and take his old place would he not get his eyes full of darkness, thus suddenly coming out of the sunlight?

He would indeed.

Now if he should be required to contend with these perpetual prisoners in 'evaluating' these shadows while his vision was still dim and before his eyes were accustomed to the dark—and this time required for habituation would not be very short—would he not provoke laughter, and would it not be said of him that he had returned from his journey aloft with his eyes ruined and that it was not worth while even to attempt the ascent? And if it were possible to lay hands on and to kill the man who tried to release them and lead them up, would they not kill him?

They certainly would, he said.[1]

[1] Plato, *The Republic*, Vol. II, trans. Paul Shorey (Cambridge, Mass.: Harvard University Press, 1935), pp. 119–129. Reprinted by permission of the publishers and The Loeb Classical Library.

## Appendix:

# METHODOLOGICAL CONSIDERATIONS

I have received many inquiries of a methodological nature from persons who are interested in future research in the area of near-death phenomena. In addition, I have given much thought to methodological questions because I myself have an interest in logic and scientific method. I have found that these questions fall generally into four areas: classification, interviewing techniques, scientific method, and proposals for future study in this area. I would like to present some of my own reflections on these matters for whatever benefit they might be to anyone who has an interest in carrying out near-death studies and also for readers who, being of a scientific or logical frame of mind, might have particular queries to make along these lines.

## I. Classification

As I have said, not everyone who has a close call with death reports having any experience at all; many report that they remember nothing whatsoever about their encounters. Some people even have an apparent clinical death and come back with no recollection of having had any conscious experience at all during that time. On the other hand, as I also mentioned, people have reported having experiences of the kind I have described even when they were not, as far as they knew, anywhere near death or even ill. Further, experiences of the kind I have dealt with have taken place under a wide spectrum of conditions which vary quite a bit with respect to what may be called (vaguely) the "closeness" with which death was approached.

Such factors could generate a certain confusion in the terminology employed in discussing these reports. Hence, I would like to propose some definitions and a classification scheme which may be of some help in lessening the confusion.

First, one might define a "near-death experience" as any conscious perceptual experience which takes place during a near-death encounter. A "near-death encounter" might in turn be defined as an event in which a person could very easily die or be killed (and even may be so close as to be believed or pronounced clinically dead) but nonetheless survives, and continues physical life.

A classification of "near-death experiences" could, I suppose, be developed from such lists of common elements of near-death experiences as the one I have set out in my earlier book. "Near-death encounters" may be classified minimally into the following kinds of situations.

A. A person finds himself in a situation in which he could very easily be killed or die, even though he subsequently escapes without injury. He reports having a subjective feeling of certainty that he would be dead very shortly. Yet, against all odds, he lives through the ordeal unharmed.

B. A person is gravely ill or injured, even to the point where his physicians give him no chance to live. Nonetheless, he never undergoes an apparent clinical death and, indeed, goes on eventually to recover.

C. A person is gravely ill or severely injured and, at some point, some of the criteria for clinical death are satisfied. For example, his heart may stop beating and/or he may stop breathing. His doctors may actually believe that he is dead. However, resuscitation procedures are immediately begun, and no one actually *pronounces* him dead. The resuscitation measures work and he lives.

D. A person is gravely ill or severely injured and, as in (C) above, at some point some of the criteria for clinical death are satisfied. Resuscitation measures are begun but do not seem to work, so they are abandoned. His doctors believe that he is dead and at some point he is actually pronounced dead. The death certificate may even be signed. However, at a later time, even *after* he has been declared dead, resuscitation measures are resumed for some reason and he is revived.

E. A person is gravely ill or severely injured and at some point some of the criteria for clinical death are satisfied. Resuscitation measures are not even begun because the case seems hopeless. His doctors believe that he is dead and at some point he is actually pronounced dead. The death certificate may even be signed. However, at a later time, even *after* he has been declared dead, resuscitation measures are begun and he is revived.

F. A person is gravely ill or severely injured and at some point some of the criteria for clinical death are satisfied. Resuscitation measures may or may not be begun, but if they are, they are abandoned, and he is believed or even pronounced dead. At a later time, however, he defies the doctors by "snapping out of it" spontaneously, without resuscitation measures being used.

I have collected examples of near-death experiences which occurred in connection with each of the types of near-death encounters listed above except for (F). That is, none of my subjects who reported an experience had it during a "death" from which he spontaneously revived. Nonetheless, spontaneous "arousals" of this nature apparently do sometimes occur. I have talked to one person who spontaneously "woke up" after having been believed dead, even though he doesn't remember having an experience in the interim.

Some might ask whether the absence of any "spontaneous recovery" cases in my collection doesn't imply that near-death experiences are merely artifacts of the technique of resuscitation —that is, something which is somehow caused by the effect on the brain or body of the procedures employed. This seems unlikely to me, for the simple reason that near-death experiences have occurred in near-death encounters of types (A) and (B) in which resuscitation measures are *not* employed.

The descriptions of types (D) and (E) raise the question of why resuscitation measures would be begun or resumed after a person has already been declared dead. The reasons have varied in the cases I have collected which fall into these categories. For example, in one case, the patient's finger was seen to twitch several minutes after he had been declared dead. Resuscitation was begun and he lived. In another, the physician involved had given up and told the nurse, "Write out the death certificate for three fifteen and I'll sign it." Shortly thereafter he decided that he just couldn't face the young son and wife of the patient involved, since he knew the family personally. He felt he just had to try again. He did, and after another extended period of resuscitation attempts the patient "came back." In yet another case, one of the medical personnel present desperately tried to talk the physician into trying again. He did, and this time the attempt worked.

With regard to types (A) through (E), I can make the following remark. In general, it seems to me that there is a progression of what one might call the depth or "completeness" of the associated near-death experiences as one goes from type (A) through type (E) near-death encounters. For example, a person who has an experience during a type (A) encounter seems typically only to report seeing his life flash before him, or only to feel that he was out of his body briefly, while those who are involved in progressively closer calls seem typically to report more of the elements which have been described. The most vivid and complete experiences I have heard took place in connection with type (D) and (E) encounters. On the other hand:

(1) This is certainly not a *necessary* correlation as far as I can tell, even in my own collection of cases. For I have met with persons who were actually believed dead and resuscitated but remember few or no elements of the experience, as well as with persons who had more complete experiences even during type (A) or (B) encounters.

(2) Establishing general correlations between type of encounter and "depth" of experience could only be done exactly through scientific studies of a type which I have not carried out, but which I will attempt to characterize later in this Appendix.

## II. Interviewing Techniques

It could be said (and truly) that the procedure of conducting interviews is a notoriously unreliable way of gathering scientific information. Thus, not surprisingly, I am often asked by interested medical professionals, "How do you go about interviewing these people?"

Now, it occurs to me in retrospect that this question is ambiguous; it has at least two distinct meanings, and I want to discuss both. The first meaning is this: "Isn't it possible that, by asking the right questions, you could plant these stories in people's minds?"

Thus formulated, this question raises a very real and interesting point. Questions *do* often suggest answers. I think it may be helpful in addressing this more precisely to make a few remarks about the concept of a question generally. In effect, questions are complex functions of language. It is probably impossible to find a question in which there is no statemental (i.e., "information-conveying") component at all, either explicitly within the verbal formulation itself or implicitly in the context in which the question is asked.

So I would say this. From a certain point of view, the technique of the interview is flawed scientifically: since it involves asking questions and questions convey information, the issue might theoretically always arise whether the information which appears to be derived from the interviewee might not originate with the interviewer through his questions or other actions.

Since I have a great interest in logic and methodology generally, my first impulse for a long time was to answer the original ambiguous question as though it had this first meaning I have just discussed. Sometimes, though, my answer seemed to leave the medical student or doctor who asked the question somehow unsatisfied. Thinking back on it, realizing as I do that many persons in the medical field themselves have a high level of anxiety about the subject of death, it occurs to me that some were probably asking a very different question indeed, namely: "How in the world do you broach such an *obscene* topic as his own clinical death with a person?"

So the original question can be resolved into at least two distinct questions, the first having a more purely logical and the second a more purely emotional impact. My interviewing techniques have been developed in response to both of these aspects.

Let me say that when I started my research it was something which apparently only a very few other persons had ever done. Consequently, no manual had been written on how to interview persons who had come back from the dead. I had to learn by experience (and, indeed, I am still learning), but I have formulated some very general rules and guidelines. I fully expect and hope that they will be modified and added to by other researchers.

The first "rule" is just this: Be sympathetic.

People are reticent to talk about these things for fear of being ridiculed or disbelieved by others. I'm sure that I would never have gotten anywhere had I used a hostile, inquisitorial kind of approach with people by trying to point out contradictions in what they say, etc.

Secondly, if you feel uncomfortable talking with people about their experiences, remember that this may well be your own fear of death coming through. I have found that persons who have been through near-death experiences seldom have the awful kind of dread of death which many of us seem to have.

Thirdly, in light of the difficulty about questions mentioned above, I think that the very best one can do is to formulate questions which emphasize the imperative function and minimize the information-conveying function as much as is possible. One should begin the interview with open-ended questions and save the more specific questions for a later point.

I always start with as neutral a question as possible, for instance, "Could you tell me what happened to you?" In a couple of cases I did ask very loaded questions. This was because the persons being interviewed were still in hospital beds recovering from the illnesses which had led to their "deaths." They were in a great deal of pain and yet obviously wanted very much to talk. I led them on a bit, I confess, because I wanted in a way to get the interviews over with as quickly as possible so that they would be more comfortable. In these cases, I asked them about whether certain

elements of the composite near-death experience
had been present in their experiences. However,
if they did not recall them, they said so. This, in
a way, gives me encouragement.

# III. Scientific Method

One difficulty in considering accounts of near-
death experiences as evidence for an afterlife is
that they are anecdotal reports. The scientific
method greatly restricts the use of human testimony as evidence. There are at least three good
reasons for this.

(1) People sometimes lie.
(2) People sometimes misremember or
misinterpret what happens to them.
(3) People sometimes have hallucinations
or delusions, especially when under stress.

Indeed, given the general fallibility of human
reporting, some might even say that such reports
as I have collected are utterly without merit.

However, some counterbalancing remarks need
to be made here. First of all, it has happened time
and time again that science has slipped up in not
listening more carefully to human testimony. For
example, until the early decades of the nineteenth
century the possibility of meteorites (rocks that
fall to the earth from outer space) was widely
dismissed and debunked by science. Still the folk
legends of stones falling from heaven persisted,

despite the insistence of scientists that this was impossible. (They argued that stones could not fall from the heavens since there were no stones in the heavens to fall.) Finally, two Princeton professors witnessed a meteorite fall and took the pieces they gathered back to their college to study.

In general, then, the dismissal of human testimony as evidence is a two-edged sword. Let's suppose that it is true that, since people often lie, misinterpret, etc., we may avoid error by disallowing human testimony as evidence. However, it must then be just as true that, since people often speak honestly and interpret correctly, we may miss the truth by refusing to heed what they say.

Furthermore, it sometimes happens that human testimony is all we have to go on at a certain time with respect to certain issues. Survival after bodily death is certainly one of these. Of course, the reports of persons who have come close to death do not constitute proof or even evidence of that issue. Still, given our curiosity, it may be that the best we can do is to ask people who have been close to death to tell us about it. If, as we have found to be the case, their independent reports agree quite well, we have a right to be impressed by that fact, even though it does not constitute proof.

Finally, the fact that a widespread phenomenon is not handled very well by our current scientific methodologies and conceptual systems should not lead us simply to dismiss it. Ideally, this fact should provoke us to try to come up with new concepts and new techniques of discovery—ones which do not contradict, but rather build upon and go beyond those to which we are accustomed.

As I have been the first to admit, the study which I have done is not strictly a "scientific" one, for many reasons. For one, the sample of subjects I have studied is not truly random, but has been selected by many factors other than chance. Also, as we saw, my study consists of anecdotal reports, which are not admissible evidence scientifically.

Some of these factors are remediable; they stem from limitations on my own resources and time. However, there are other problems arising from the very nature of the subject matter under investigation here which would make it exceedingly difficult, if not impossible, to carry out an unquestionably scientific study under adequately controlled experimental conditions. These problems are both moral and procedural. Obviously, we can't put statistically significant numbers of people into a state of clinical death in order to be able to record their impressions upon a hoped-for resuscitation!

The actual clinical situations involved are not controlled experimental environments, but rather medical emergencies. The first duty of a physician and the other medical personnel in such circumstances is, and ought only to be, to give therapy to the patient, to try to revive him. It is not their duty to perform experiments related to the nature or validity of near-death experiences.

It seems that the only thing that would be clearly within the limits of moral acceptability would be to collect data, in effect, after the fact.

Data quite often come into existence in the course of resuscitation attempts, not because a conscious attempt has been made to collect them for scientific purposes, but rather as the more or less secondary result of the therapeutic and/or diagnostic measures taken. For example, clinical records often may show why a person "died" or came close to death, how long he was in this state, how he was brought back from it, what his first responses were upon being brought back, what drugs were administered to him, etc. Also, "harder" data might exist in the form of any tracings from EEG or EKG machines used, recorded temperature and blood pressure readings, results of any laboratory tests which were done before or after the emergency, and so on. It is conceivable that advances in resuscitation technology or instrumentation might make such data even more reliable and easier to come by in the near future.

# IV. Preliminary Suggestions for Future Research

Granted the availability of data of the type mentioned above, and possibly of other kinds, how can near-death experiences be studied? One possibility is the formation of an inter-disciplinary study group in which interested representatives from many fields will work together. Among the fields which can be represented are medicine, physiology, pharmacology, philosophy, psychology, psychiatry, anthropology, comparative religion, theology, and the ministry.

A group of this nature could address itself to a large number of tasks. Among them are the following.

A. Examples of near-death experiences could be collected in a more systematic and organized way. For example, doctors and hospital staff members could be contacted and requested to ask patients whom they resuscitate whether they had experiences and to report the response. Or, the request could be to permit a team of investigators to approach the patient and ascertain whether he had an experience. Note: The cases in which no experience at all was reported would be important, too, for the sake of comparative studies.

B. Clinical records of the "after the fact" type described above could be searched out and compiled for as many of the near-death experiences as possible. This could be valuable as corroboration that the person who describes an experience did "die" or come near death. In addition, this data might make it possible to compile a more reliable statistical cross section of the medical status of persons having experiences and help to reveal whether there is any pattern to be found with respect to cause of death, age at time of the experience, methods of resuscitation employed, and so forth. A statistically better cor-

relation than I have been able to make might
be established between the length of time a
subject is in a physiological crisis and the
depth of his experience.

C. A search might be made for instances in
which independent corroboration of a very
persuasive type exists. "Ideal" cases of this
type might be constructed, for example, along
lines similar to these.

(1) In an emergency room, an individual,
Mr. A, is being treated for a severe medical
crisis by doctors and medical personnel. Since
his treatment has continued for some time,
there has been adequate time for instrumentation to be carefully and correctly set up,
so that the medical team can monitor his
status. Accordingly, gauges are giving information about his blood pressure and respiration while an EKG monitors his heart function and an EEG is keeping the personnel
informed of the activity of his brain. Precisely
at a certain time, which is carefully recorded
by those on hand, Mr. A undergoes a cardiac
and respiratory arrest, and this is both clinically apparent and recorded on the instrumentation. Someone there both witnesses
and records that Mr. A's pupils dilate and
that his body temperature begins to fall. Resuscitation attempts are begun immediately
and, after a precisely timed interval, succeed.
Mr. A recovers.

Soon thereafter, Mr. A tells his physicians

that he had a fantastic experience while he was "dead"; that he seemed to get out of his body and to witness the resuscitation attempts from another point of view. He reports that while in this state he left the room entirely and went to another place where he witnessed an unusual event taking place, which he proceeds to describe in detail.

Not only do the medical personnel agree that Mr. A's account of their actions in resuscitating him is accurate, but an immediate check establishes that the event which he says he witnessed while outside of the room *did* take place almost exactly where and as he said it did. Further, it can be established that the event took place at the precise time when Mr. A is known to have been in a state of clinical death, as supported by flat EEG and EKG tracings.

(2) Suppose two or more persons undergo a clinical "death" simultaneously and are resuscitated. This could happen, for example, in the course of a mass accident of some kind, or if two or more persons just happened to "die" in the same hospital at the same time. Suppose further that they were to both report as soon as they came back—while still isolated from one another—that they had communicated with one another while in the out-of-body state. The content of this alleged communication could be collected from both independently while they were still isolated

from each other. If this checked out, it would certainly be significant and interesting.

Neither of the two types of cases described above, however, would necessarily constitute proof of life after death. Extrasensory perception could be a possible explanation of any cases of these two "ideal" types. Someone could always raise the possibility that the subjects were able to observe what they did, not by actually leaving their bodies, but by telepathically picking up the thoughts of observers who were physically at the scene.

I am not suggesting that it is likely that researchers will come up with cases which are as perfect as the ones outlined above. I do suggest that investigators formulate a series of theoretical models. Using them as a standard, the investigators could compare actual cases to the modes and to one another and devise a "yardstick" for classifying actual encounters.

D. Investigators trained in psychology might carry out in-depth interviews with subjects who came near death. Valuable clues might be revealed as to how the patient's experience changed him, to what degree his interpretation of it was shaped by his emotional makeup and background, and so on. Comparisons of the results could reveal how persons reporting near-death experiences differ among themselves and if they differ from the population as a whole.

E. Separate elements of near-death experiences may well have to be studied and/or explained separately. For example, suppose that the "buzzing" noise people report at the moments near death turned out to have a particular phsysiological explanation. It would not follow that any other elements in the experience—say, the encounter with relatives and friends who had died before—would have the same type of explanation.

F. An extensive search could be made for cases of near-death experiences from contexts outside that of modern Western society. The aid of anthropologists might be enlisted in collecting near-death experiences from the members of very different cultures. A careful review of historical literature might turn up instances from our own Western tradition. An expert in the field of comparative religion might be able to point out parallels in the many religions of the world. The possibilities are endless.

G. Persons who have had near-death experiences could be brought together in groups to discuss their experiences among themselves. I have done this many times now and find it has many advantages. Until now most people who have had this experience have thought they were all alone or that their cases were so rare they would never find someone else who had had a similar experience.

This impression is certainly dispelled intellectually and emotionally in a group. Also, the effability gap is partly bridged. People say that for the first time they feel they have met someone who really understands and empathizes, despite the limitations of language. At the close of a group experience of this type, one man enthused, "That was the most fantastic evening of my life. I was discussing things I usually can't even talk about." I have found that as an observer in these groups I have been able to understand in a better way than before what a near-death experience may be like.

I would like to give two pointers here. A group of three persons who have had this experience is about the optimum size, it seems to me. Also, it can be helpful to have the spouses of the participants present. They have often themselves had trouble understanding this experience of their wife or husband, and having another person tell about a similar experience might help.

H. Finally, I feel that close attention should be paid to the arguments of those who see this phenomenon as explicable in terms of natural causes and scientific concepts with which we are already familiar—for example, residual electrical activity of the brain. For, it goes without saying that natural science has brought us a long way in our understanding of the universe.

At the same time, I think that one should avoid the temptation to accept simple-minded natural explanations without putting them to any sort of test. I have heard many people make remarks to the effect that it is just "obvious" that the explanation of near-death phenomena is, for example, cerebral anoxia (that is, loss of oxygen supply to the brain). It is quite easy to come up with any number of possible natural explanations of this type off the top of one's head. What is lacking, I would suggest, is any particular experimental demonstration that any given explanation of this type is correct. As I pointed out in *Life After Life*, what makes me doubt simplistic explanations of this type is that I can find certain near-death experiences in which each explanation which has ever been proposed to me just doesn't fit the facts or situation surrounding those particular experiences.

After all, there is a difference between "explaining" something and merely "explaining it away." The latter involves reducing an apparently new phenomenon to an old one, or saying that the new is really just a special case of phenomena with which we are already familiar (or think we are). It seems to me that we should always be at least open to the possibility that what seem to be new phenomena are true anomalies—items or facts which just do not fit into the structure of previously articulated world views. For it is certainly just this openness to the occurrence of anomalies in our experience which has historically been one of the greatest incentives to the advancement of human understanding.

# V. Some Concluding Remarks

Let me close this section on methodology with a few random remarks which might be of value to any future researchers of this phenomenon. First, I think that researchers should avoid the tendency to dismiss near-death experiences as unworthy topics for research just because certain elements in them conflict with dearly held assumptions about the nature of the world.

I admit that near-death experiences contain aspects which, from our present perspective, are completely incomprehensible. For example, apparent inconsistencies arise regarding time. The contemporary Western view of time is that it is an intimate feature of the physical universe, that it flows forever in a linear fashion. Yet people who come back from near-death experiences assert that "time stood still."

I don't have any answers for people who ask questions about these apparent anomalies. Nonetheless, as I am sure quite a few physicists and philosophers would agree, the common sense concept of time generates many paradoxes just in itself, regardless of the occurrence of near-death visions. The additional dilemmas posed by a consideration of near-death experiences are just a drop in the bucket.

I also caution researchers to avoid the tendency to assume that just because someone has been "dead," and has had an experience, he must know everything about what happens on the other side. No one has come back feeling that he was infallible or omniscient with regard to the afterlife because of his experience. Most have expressed genuine bafflement about many of the things they went through. In other words, if someone is fallible here, before he has his experience, there is no reason to assume that he is going to be infallible after he returns from "death."

Finally, it would more likely advance our understanding of the human mind if persons who are interested in doing research on near-death experiences would tackle only one aspect at a time. I feel that a huge research project geared to the aim of proving that there is life after death through study of near-death experiences would likely be ill-conceived and, at the current level of our understanding, overly ambitious. My own feeling is that, *within the context of science alone,* there may never be a proof of life after death.

On the other hand, I believe that a large number of individual research projects, each one set up with the aim of testing some particular, more limited experimental hypothesis, would be likely to yield scientifically usable data about near-death experiences. Further, I believe that possibly the end result of the accumulation of particular bits of knowledge through these individual, painstaking attempts would be a fading away of the issue of whether there is life after death, without a single, dramatic scientific proof ever being given.

Let me illustrate what I mean by an analogy. Though most of us believe in the existence of atoms, there never was—to my knowledge—a single, dramatic proof of this. Rather, what happened seems to have been a long, historical development of thought relating to these hypothetical entities. Even hundreds of years before Christ, Greek philosophers such as Democritus had conceived of an atomic theory of matter. They postulated the existence of minute, "indivisible" particles of matter. They did this partly on the basis of abstract, deductive, and metaphysical reasoning, but partly also on the basis of their own empirical observations of various natural phenomena such as diffusion and the imperceptibly gradual wearing away of large objects. Through centuries of development, during which the concept of the atom was altered and techniques for the verification of its existence were correspondingly modified, the atomic theory has slowly come to be widely accepted.

I believe it lies within the realm of possibility that, in a similar fashion, almost everyone may eventually come to accept intellectually, even without definite proof, that there is another dimension of existence into which the soul passes at death. Remember that it is our own anxiety about whether death is final which shows through when we challenge a person who has had such an experience to *prove* that there is life after death.

Most people who have had near-death experiences don't seem interested in proving it to other people. One woman psychiatrist who had a near-death experience told me, "People who have had these experiences *know*. People who haven't should *wait*."

# BIBLIOGRAPHY

## Near-Death Experiences
## and Parallels

Barrett, William. *Death-Bed Visions*. London: Methuen & Co., 1926.

Bede. *A History of the English Church and People*, trans. Leo Sherley-Price. Harmondsworth, England: Penguin Books, 1968.

Canning, Raymond R. "Mormon Return-From-The-Dead Stories." *Utah Academy Proceedings*, XLII (1965). Cited in *The Sociology of Death*, by Glenn M. Vernon. New York: The Ronald Press Co., 1970, pp. 64–65.

Delacour, Jean-Baptiste. *Glimpses of the Beyond*. New York: Delacorte Press, 1973.

De Quincey, Thomas. *Confessions of An English Opium Eater With Its Sequels Suspiria De Profundis and The English Mail-Coach*, ed. Malcolm Elwin. London: Macdonald & Co., 1956.

Dobson, M., et al. "Attitudes and Long Term Adjustment of Patients Surviving Cardiac Arrest." *British Medical Journal*, Vol. 3 (1971), pp. 207–212.

Hamilton, Edith, and Huntington Cairns, eds. *The*

*Collected Dialogues of Plato*. Bollingen Series LXXI. New York: Pantheon Books, 1961.

Hunter, R. C. A. "On The Experience Of Nearly Dying." *American Journal of Psychiatry*, 124 (1967), pp. 122–126.

Jackson, Kenneth H. *A Celtic Miscellany*. London, England: Routledge & Kegan Paul, Ltd., 1971.

James, William. *The Varieties of Religious Experience*. New York: New American Library, 1958.

Jung, C. G. *Memories, Dreams, and Reflections*, ed. Aniela Jaffé and trans. Richard and Clara Winston. New York: Vintage Books, 1965.

Kubler-Ross, Elisabeth. *On Death and Dying*. New York: Macmillan, 1969.

Neihardt, John G. *Black Elk Speaks*. New York: Pocket Books, 1972.

Noyes, Russell. "The Experience of Dying." *Psychiatry*, Vol. 35 (1972), pp. 174–184.

Noyes, Russell, and Roy Kletti. "Depersonalization In The Face Of Life-Threatening Danger: A Description." *Psychiatry*, Vol. 39 (1976), pp. 19–27.

Osis, Karl. *Deathbed Observations by Physicians and Nurses*. Parapsychological Monographs, No. 3. New York: Parapsychology Foundation, 1961.

Osis, Karl. "What Do The Dying See." *Newsletter of the American Society For Psychical Research*, 24 (Winter 1975).

Pandey, Carol. "The Need For The Psychological Study of Clinical Death." *Omega*, Vol. 2 (1971), pp. 1–9.

Ritchie, George. *Return From Tomorrow*. Lincoln, Virginia: Chosen Books, (to be published in November 1977).

Tylor, Edward B. *Primitive Culture*, Vol. II. New York: Henry Holt and Company, 1874.

Uekshuell, K. "Unbelievable For Many, But Actually A True Occurrence." *Moscow Journal* (late 19th Century). Translated and reprinted in *Orthodox Life*, Vol. 26, No. 4 (1976), pp. 1–36.

## ABOUT THE AUTHOR

RAYMOND A. MOODY is married and has two sons. He has studied and taught philosophy extensively, taking a special interest in ethics, logic and the philosophy of language. After having taught philosophy, he continued his studies in medicine and decided to become a psychiatrist in order to teach the philosophy of medicine in a medical school. During this time, he studied the phenomena of survival of bodily death, lecturing to various nursing and medical groups. In *Reflections On Life After Life*, Dr. Moody continues his investigation of life after dying. He is presently doing research in the area of humor therapy.

# SPECIAL
# MONEY SAVING
# OFFER

Now you can have an up-to-date listing of Bantam's hundreds of titles plus take advantage of our unique and exciting bonus book offer. A special offer which gives you the opportunity to purchase a Bantam book for only 50¢. Here's how!

By ordering any five books at the regular price per order, you can also choose any other single book listed (up to a $4.95 value) for just 50¢. Some restrictions do apply, but for further details why not send for Bantam's listing of titles today!

Just send us your name and address plus 50¢ to defray the postage and handling costs.

BANTAM BOOKS, INC.
Dept. FC, 414 East Golf Road, Des Plaines, Ill 60016

Mr./Mrs./Miss/Ms. _____
(please print)

Address _____

City_____ State_____ Zip_____

FC—3/84